Other than War

The American Military
Experience and Operations
in the Post-Cold War Decade

FRANK N. SCHUBERT

Joint History Office
Office of the Chairman of the Joint Chiefs of Staff
Washington, DC • 2013

Executive Summary

The almost 300 military deployments between 1989 and 2001 appear at a glance to be a bewildering assortment of domestic and overseas missions that overtaxed the US military and confirmed theories of global chaos. "Other than War," Dr. Frank N. Schubert's analysis of the American military experience and operations in the post-Cold War decade, demonstrates that the operations were neither as diffuse nor as numerous as they first appeared. Instead of looking at hundreds of disparate operations ranging the globe, grouping common operations in specific regions significantly reduces the overall total and clarifies the focus of the deployments. Moreover, the nature of the operations comports with a long US military tradition of law enforcement, disaster relief, humanitarian assistance, and nation building as well as constabulary operations, including pacification and so-called small wars.

The pattern of operations seems perplexing in part because they were listed as individual responses to separate emergencies and not conceptualized as parts of broader campaigns. Stability operations in the Balkans and Iraq, for example, assigned new names to iterations or single tasks of the continuing operations and obscured the fact that these were two regional campaigns, not almost 100 separate ones. The profusion of names also appeared in the continuing drug enforcement and migrant interdiction operations in the Caribbean and Panama. Humanitarian operations during the decade responded to an average of three disasters per year, half in the Western Hemisphere where autumn hurricanes, spring floods along the Missouri and Mississippi, and summer fires in the western part of the United States were almost predictable events. Other deployments included non-combatant evacuation (NEO) operations and support of travel by senior executive branch officials.

Experts were misled by the variety of names and the numbers of military personnel involved in deployments relative to the size of the total overseas forces. In any one year, fewer than five percent of US military personnel stationed overseas were deployed on operations and most of them were in the Balkans or Southwest Asia, namely Iraq.

Major units in demand were not conventional combat formations but military police, engineers, civil affairs, and Special Forces as well as specialized aircraft for reconnaissance, surveillance, and air defense suppression. The Army's and Air Force's reliance on reservists offset the operational tempo at least to some degree.

The pattern of the late 20th century may reemerge after the United States departs from Afghanistan. Containing Iran's nuclear ambitions recalls containing Iraq; small, specialized units, not conventional forces, will continue the hunt for terrorists; humanitarian, drug interdiction, and disaster relief missions will continue to demand military resources. All operations were unique, to be sure, but they also evolved in an operational, institutional, and historical context that help explain their purpose and define their character.

Foreword

Established during World War II to advise the President on the strategic direction of the armed forces of the United States, the Joint Chiefs of Staff (JCS) continued in the postwar era to play a significant role in the development of national policy. Knowledge of JCS relations with the President, the National Security Council, and the Secretary of Defense in the years since World War II is essential to an understanding of their current responsibilities. An account of their activities in peacetime and during times of crises provides, moreover, an important account of the military history of the United States. For these reasons, the Joint Chiefs of Staff directed that an official history be written for the record. Its value for instructional purposes, for the orientation of officers newly assigned to the JCS organization, and as a source of information for staff studies will be readily recognized.

In this study, Dr. Frank N. Schubert examines the almost 300 US military deployments that occurred between 1989 and 2001. At the time the large number of these deployments appeared to overtax the US military and support theories of global chaos. His analysis of the American military experience and operations in the post-Cold War decade demonstrates that the operations were neither as diffuse nor as numerous as first thought. Instead of looking at hundreds of disparate operations ranging the globe, grouping common operations in specific regions significantly reduces the overall total and clarifies the focus of the deployments. Moreover, the nature of the operations comports with a long US military tradition of law enforcement, disaster relief, humanitarian assistance, and nation building as well as constabulary operations, including pacification and so-called small wars.

Ms. Susan Carroll prepared the Index, and Ms. Penny Norman prepared the manuscript for publication. This volume is an official publication of the Joint Chiefs of Staff but, inasmuch as the text has not been considered by the Joint Chiefs of Staff, it must be construed as descriptive only and does not constitute the official position of the Joint Chiefs of Staff on any subject.

Washington, DC
January 2013

John F. Shortal
Brigadier General, USA (Ret.)
Director for Joint History

Preface

This book originated in the complex post-Cold War operational environment of the 1990s. In the autumn of 1996, while working in the Joint
History Office, I received my first request for a list of current operations from
a joint staff action officer. Before the year ended, one of the chairman's speech-
writers asked for an accurate list of operations and deployments. No such
list existed at that time, so I undertook to build one. For the next five years, I
accumulated data for operations that had already been completed, tried to keep
current on operations in progress, and sorted out the names of too many operations whose names started with "Provide," "Restore," and "Support." All the
while, requests for such information continued, reinforcing my confidence that
this was a useful undertaking.

Judging from the requests for data and my own sense of the kinds of information that were needed, I sought to track a wide range of operation elements,
from the identity of the unified command responsible for a mission to the
number of casualties incurred. Other items of interest included the identity
and nature of deployed units, the names of commanders, the duration of an
operation, the nature of the mission, the involvement of contractors, non-governmental organizations and other government agencies, and the dollar cost of
the operation. As Gerald Turley wrote early in 2001, the data was vital for an
appreciation of the wide range of possible scenarios, for an understanding of
economic, cultural, and geographic aspects of operations, and even for mod-
eling and simulation. "Given the large number of incidents since 1945," he
went on, "it is surprising that there is no established database or repository for
MOOTW [Military Operations other than War]; nor is there a single location
where historical information (i.e., dates, locations, types of actions, and lessons
learned) is stored."[1]

Not all of the desired data became available for all of the operations. A
member of a Department of Defense working group seeking to create its
own database correctly noted in October 2000 that my collection was indeed
"uneven and incomplete." Moreover, it would always remain imperfect, for a
variety of reasons, among them the quality and nature of record-keeping and
the classification of some documentation. But I continued to share my data base
with any Department of Defense Office that expressed interest. A number in
fact did, including elements of the office of the Secretary of Defense, the Joint
Staff, and the service staffs, I also provided copies to the Department of De-

fense client of any contractor who asked about the project.

The assembly and examination of the data suggested connections among the missions themselves as well as between them and two centuries of American military operations. This essay seeks to identify and explain these connections, to try to make sense of what some claimed was a mass of diffuse and unrelated missions, and to consider what the decade's work portended for the future. It is based mainly on the data base itself, along with my reading in the professional and scholarly literature of the 1990s. Now that the wars in Afghanistan and Iraq are winding down, Marine General Anthony Zinni's prediction on operations to come—"We're going to be doing things like humanitarian operations, consequence management, peacekeeping and peace enforcement ... operations other than war. These are our future."—may have renewed validity.[2]

As might be clear by now, I undertook the creation of the data base on which this essay is largely based without an official directive to do so. Dr. David A. Armstrong (BG, USA, Ret.), who then headed the Joint History Office, saw the merit in what I was doing and supported me in the preparation of the documentation and in the writing of the essay itself. I am grateful for his encouragement, guidance, and friendship. Ensign Nathaniel Morgan, USN, had a major role in shaping the data base on which this essay is based. While I was trying to decide how to go about this at the end of 1996, Ensign Morgan was assigned to the office on a short-term basis while awaiting a more permanent assignment. His technical skill was indispensible in setting up a framework in Microsoft's Access database program. By the time he left the office I was able to store the data in a sortable manner. He is as much responsible to the emergence of a usable product as I am. Others who facilitated and influenced this work included Norman Polmar, Edgar Raines, Erwin Schmidl, John M. Gates, John Pitts, James T. Matthews, Peg Nigra, Kent Beck, Maren Leed, and most recently Dr. John F. Shortal (BG, USA, Ret.) the present Director for Joint History, Edward J. Drea, and Penny Norman. Thank you all.

Mount Vernon, Virginia

Frank N. Schubert
January 2013

Contents

Chapter 1
An Overview

The period from the end of the Cold War in 1989-1991 to the attacks on the United States by terrorists on 11 September 2001 spanned little more than a decade. American military operations during that time ranged the globe and included peace operations, humanitarian expeditions of various kinds, and counter-drug efforts. Carried out without the coherent framework provided by the Cold War, the missions of the 1990s were many, diverse, and diffuse, characteristics that sometimes created an impression of heavy activity, even overwork. The common thread among these post-Cold War missions, from the intervention in Panama during December 1989 to soldiers and Marines fighting forest fires in the western United States in the summer of 2000, was that they rarely resembled conventional warfare.

The collapse of the Soviet Union had left the United States the world's preeminent military power. Yet despite the fact that there was no substantial conventional threat to the country, in the ensuing decade the American armed forces seemed extremely busy with operations that sent American military personnel to places far from their homes and families. These activities included stability operations, which were missions "characterised [sic] by intra state conflict between two or more factions divided over issues such as ethnicity, nationality and religion," and "encompassing peace building, peacekeeping, peace making, and peace enforcement."[1] The decade also brought humanitarian assignments and responses to disasters and political crises. Some missions, such as the series of operations in Southwest Asia and in the Balkans, were long and costly. Others, such as the evacuation of American civilians from countries in sub-Saharan Africa, were quick and relatively inexpensive. Overall, hundreds of operational names were applied to an apparently bewildering array of deployments.[2]

Similar and highly optimistic names, such as **Provide Assistance, Provide Comfort, Provide Hope, Provide Promise, Provide Refuge, Provide Relief,** and **Provide Transition**, abounded.[3] In the Balkans, where the proliferation of operational names presented almost as great a challenge to understanding as the competing claims and grievances of the aggrieved parties, at least six operational designations started with "Decisive," four with "Deliberate," and four with "Determined." Five other names began with "Joint." If their names were frequently similar, the locations of the operations were all over the map, with 253 deployments of various sizes, composition, and duration, including about 110 to Latin America (44%), 43 to Europe (17%), 35 to Asia (14%), 29 to Africa (11%), 21 in North America (8%), and 15 in Oceania (6%).[4]

While joint operations responded to a wide range of emergencies and were conducted around the world, there were several regions in which large numbers of joint operations took place in response to prolonged regional crises. Occurring in the same region and in response to a common threat, these groups of operations closely resembled the campaigns of conventional wars and can be thought of in those terms. Because they were made up of individual responses to separate emergencies, rather than part of a single plan aimed at achieving a sequence of objectives leading to a decisive goal, such campaigns often contained operations of multiple types and phases, frequently with separate names. Consequently, the pattern of operations frequently seemed bewildering, in part because of the large number and dispersion of activities as well as the profusion of names, and in part because of its sharp contrast with the single focus of the Cold War.

The conflict with the Soviet Union had concentrated the attention and expectations of American policymakers and planners and the American public on a single large-scale conflict within the framework formed by the North Atlantic Treaty Organization and Warsaw Pact alliances.[5] At the same time, the two superpowers had exercised some control of their allies and client states. Consequently, to observers accustomed to the relatively static background of the Cold War, the large number, frequency, and diverse nature of the activities demanded by the post–Cold War environment often seemed to impose unusually high demands on the United States military.

Yet when aggregated into functional or regional clusters, the operations of the post–Cold War decade were not as diverse or numerous as they appeared. Some groups reflected traditional American interests, such as activities in the Caribbean; others, such as humanitarian operations and noncombatant evacuations in sub-Saharan Africa, did not. The two biggest and most costly bodies of operations involved decade-long efforts to contain the regime of Saddam Hussein in Iraq and to bring stability to what had once been Yugoslavia. Seen in retrospect, these two groupings closely resemble the campaigns of earlier conflicts.

Viewed from a longer historical perspective, the operations during the decade did not represent new departures. Throughout its history the American military has engaged in peace operations, nationbuilding, humanitarian work, and law enforcement. While the end of the Cold War removed a structure which had given coherence to and, to some degree, constrained American operations for nearly two generations, missions carried out in the 1990s were not a radical departure from the experience of the more distant past.

At times, the missions of the first post–Cold War decade seemed new and unprecedented; peace operations certainly appeared to represent a new feature of the post-Cold War environment. Nevertheless, as Thomas Mockaitis points out,[6] the description of peace operations published in the Army's field manual on the subject strongly resembled a depiction of Cold War-era insurgency:

> Peace operations may often take place in environments that are less well-defined than in war. The identity of belligerents may be uncertain and the relationship between a specific operation and a campaign plan may be less clear than would normally be the case in combat .... Loosely organized groups of irregulars, terrorists, or other conflicting segments of a population may predominate. These segments will attempt to capitalize on perceptions of disaffection within the population.[7]

As much as the operational pattern of the 1990s appeared distinctly different, it contained strong elements of continuity with the past.

During the 1990s, it became clear that the forces in greatest demand were not the major combat formations that dominated the Cold War structure of American forces. Military police, medical units, engineers, air transport, and surveillance aircraft were in very high demand; armor and infantry divisions and carrier battle groups were not. In response, the military services sought to adjust to the reality of post-Cold War operations; they changed their doctrines, organizations, and deployment policies. Many of these changes were being implemented when the terrorist attacks of September 2001 gave the American military a new operational focus which, nevertheless, had some of the 1990s requirements and concerns.

Although United States forces were busy throughout the 1990s, they were involved in only a small portion of the world's disasters and armed conflicts. According to the Emergency Events Database, developed and maintained by the Centre for Research on the Epidemiology of Disasters of the School of Public Health at Louvain Catholic University in Brussels, Belgium, during the years 1990 through 1999, 4,864 disasters were reported. This figure included events in which at least ten people were reported killed and 100 people were reported affected and which were followed by an appeal for international assistance, the declaration of a state of emergency, or both. Aggregated by continent, the worldwide total included 798 disasters in Africa, 1,088 in the Americas, 2,071 in Asia, 734 in Europe, and 172 in Oceania.[8] In addition to these thousands of events, there were numerous armed conflicts, 98 in the seven years from 1990 through 1996, including seven clashes between states and 91 between factions within a single country or political entity.[9]

There was much about the operational environment of the 1990s that had ample precedent in the American military tradition. During the 1920s and 1930s, the

United States armed forces lacked a major war to fight. Nevertheless, the twenty-year period was a busy one for both the Army and the Navy, with a wide range of operations in the United States and outside the country in the Western Hemisphere and the coastal zones of East Asia. These ranged from long-term stability operations in the Caribbean—Nicaragua, the Dominican Republic, and Haiti—to quelling domestic disturbances and managing massive water resource development programs that gave employment to thousands during the Depression.

Still earlier, in the period between the Civil War and the war with Spain in 1898, the United States did not face a major threat. Yet the American armed forces were busy with operations over much of the country, especially the vast reaches of the trans-Mississippi West. These operations included campaigns against Indians—small, grueling conflicts that disrupted long periods of "inter-positional peacekeeping," that put the Army between the growing number of civilian settlements and natives whose lives they were disrupting and changing. The frontier Army also responded to calls for help from civilian communities afflicted by floods, blizzards, droughts, even infestations of grasshoppers, as well as to labor disputes that grew in number, size, and scope as the twentieth century approached. Elements of the Army surveyed and built roads, protected telegraph lines, laid out river crossings, and protected overland commerce and migrations. Meanwhile, the Navy was also busy with numerous operations designed to protect Americans and their commerce.

Overall, from the earliest days of the Republic, operations such as those identified above characterized the role of American forces during long periods of peace. As Andrew Birtle, an Army historian specializing in small wars and counterinsurgency operations, noted at the end of the twentieth century, "In the century and a half between the founding of the Republic and America's entry into World War II, the Army conducted explorations, governed territories, guarded national parks, engaged in public works, provided disaster relief, quelled domestic disturbances, and supported American foreign policy short of engaging in open warfare."[10] Meanwhile, the Navy and Marines were busy with operations designed to protect Americans and their commerce; their involvement in enforcing freedom of the seas had begun early in the nineteenth century.

In the nineteenth and twentieth centuries, there was also combat, much of it in the context of "unconventional conflicts against a bewildering array of irregulars, from American Indians to Bolshevik partisans."[11] Although increasingly large in size and scope, in the period before the Cold War conventional wars involving American forces were relatively few: the war with Britain (1812-1815), the war with Mexico (1846-1848), the Civil War (1861-1865), the war with Spain (1898), and the two World Wars. As Birtle noted, the American military tradition involved a "continuous engagement in operations other than war."[12]

Chapter 2
Nineteenth Century Operations

Much of the American military tradition is a study in dualities. One dichotomy, the regular versus the citizen-soldier, is frequently examined.[1] Another, the expansion for war of a very small peacetime armed force and the drastic contraction of the force following hostilities, is also generally known and appreciated.[2] But another duality, the two aspects of the operational history of the American military, is less widely understood. On one side are wars against foreign enemies and planning and preparation for them, efforts widely considered to be the *raison d'etre* of the US armed forces. Procurement programs, training, doctrine, and organization all focus on this aspect of military operations. In the year 2000, this view of war against foreign enemies as the proper role of the American military extended to senior officials of both major political parties.[3] A Deputy Assistant Secretary of Defense in the Democratic administration divided the responsibilities of the military into fighting wars, a core function, and civil support, a secondary one.[4] On the same day during a nationally televised debate, George W. Bush, then the Republican presidential candidate, said: "I don't think our troops ought to be used for what's called nation building. I think our troops ought to be used to fight and win a war."[5]

In spite of the apparent consensus represented by these views, American military history reflects two operational aspects, one that has involved wars against foreign enemies and another that involved a variety of operations, including law enforcement, disaster relief, humanitarian assistance, and nation-building. These types of tasks, sometimes referred to as *gendarme* or constabulary operations, include pacification operations and "small wars," later called counterinsurgency or contingency operations.[6]

In carrying out a diverse array of missions and responsibilities, United States forces operated in the tradition established nearly two thousand years ago by the Army of Imperial Rome. On the far frontiers of the empire, in Britain, across Germany along the Rhine and through the Carpathian basin on both sides of the Danube, in Arabia and North Africa, the Roman army carried out both conventional warfare and gendarme missions. The latter included guarding the frontiers against barbarian attacks; battling outlaws within the empire; preparing maps and surveying the land; building forts, roads, bridges, and aqueducts; supervising construction projects and labor details in mines and quarries;

and digging canals and dams. Like soldiers of other eras, the legionaries hated such assignments. The Roman historian Tacitus noted that in Germany the men "complained about the hardness of the work and specifically about building ramparts, digging ditches, foraging, collecting timber and firewood, and all the other camp tasks ...."[7] Nevertheless, they carried out their orders and major construction activities: "Thousands of legionaries ... became instant quarrymen, masons, brickmakers, limemakers and tilers; hundreds of sailors became bargees and lightermen." According to British historian Derek Williams, they served as "... the *gendarmerie* of the empire's edges and keepers of its gates; not only policing the frontier and administering the formalities at checkpoints and crossings, but also defending it and retaliating to trouble."[8]

In the course of carrying out their duties, the soldiers of the Roman Empire protected and nurtured the development of settlement, created a demand in the outlying parts of the empire for manufactured goods and farm produce, spent their salaries on local entertainment and products, and generally encouraged the development of towns and commerce. Like the Roman army which, as Stephen Drummond observed, represented "the dominant institutional factor in the development of the frontier," the United States Army on the frontier was "the 'right arm' of the federal government in its nineteenth-century expansionist policies."[9] In either case, an organization devoted exclusively to preparation for and fighting foreign wars could not have made such a dramatic and pervasive impact on regional development.

From the earliest days of the American republic, its military forces made vital contributions to the development of the nation's frontier regions, carrying out contingency operations traditionally known as "shows of force." The longest-standing variety, which eventually came to be called "operations of interposition," sought to protect American lives and property by placing military forces between threatened citizens and the danger. In fact, the United States Army, "the child of the frontier," according to Robert M. Utley, was born of the operational requirement emerging from conflict between settlers and native peoples who resisted encroachment on their lands and the inability of local volunteer organizations to cope with the problem.[10] This problem became clear in the autumn of 1791, when a coalition of tribes attacked the camp of Major General Arthur J. St. Clair. When the Indians withdrew, more than 600 American militiamen were dead in the worst Indian war disaster to befall American military forces. As Utley noted, "The Indian rout of [Brigadier General Josiah] Harmer and St. Clair so dramatically exposed the inadequacies of the militia as to give birth to the Regular Army, a contribution of the militia to US military history of no small significance, however negative."[11]

The American Army's major operations against Indians in the pre-Civil War years are marked by eight campaign streamers covering the years from

1790 to 1858 and involving operations from Florida to the Great Lakes.[12] In this period there were brief conventional foreign wars against the British in 1812-1815 and against Mexico in 1846-1848. The pre-Civil War Army—"over-worked, underfunded, and dispersed among many small posts," according to Utley—spent the bulk of its time policing the nation's ever-changing western boundary." Soldiers enforced laws and treaties, explored and later policed newly acquired territories, punished aggressive hostiles, and regulated contact between citizens of the Republic and Indians. In the course of carrying out these duties "by offering security or the appearance of it, together with a market for labor and produce, they encouraged further settlement."[13]

During the period between the Mexican War and the Civil War, both the Army and the Navy made significant contributions to national development well outside their primary missions of providing defense against foreign enemies. The Army worked largely within the boundaries of the United States, mapping, surveying, protecting migrating citizens, and expanding the nation's borders, while documenting the fauna, flora, native peoples, and providing places on expeditions for scholars eager to examine the new country. The Navy made its contributions outside of the United States, through scientific and technical expeditions and data collections of wide-ranging impact, with maps of winds and currents that proved of vital importance to commercial mariners, as well as expeditions to regions of great interest to scientists, including the Amazon, the Isthmus of Panama, and the Arctic Ocean. The eagle of American expansion screamed on the high seas as well as on the continent.[14]

In the years before the Civil War, US Navy operations resembled in many respects the Army's police operations in North America. These took place on foreign shores—in Latin America, Asia, the South Pacific, and along the Mediterranean. They sometimes went beyond interposition to become "operations of intervention," intended to restore order, quell insurrection, or impose punitive measures for harm done to American nationals. In at least twenty-four instances between the War of 1812 and the American Civil War, sailors and Marines landed either to protect Americans, their property and commerce in places remote to the United States or to punish those who had abused American citizens. Sometimes, they landed to shield third-country nationals and their property.[15] Historian Kenneth Hagan saw these operations as manifestations of a global pattern of deployment. While keeping an eye on Barbary pirates, the small American Navy cruised the Pacific to protect American trade and whaling, watched over the China trade in the seas south of India, and hunted pirates and slavers off the coast of Africa, in the West Indies, in the Gulf of Mexico, and along the southern coast of the United States.[16] Once widely known as "gunboat diplomacy," these operations long ago faded into disuse and by the 1990s were replaced by non-combatant evacuation operations, termed "NEOs," which resulted in very brief use of forces to extract, rather than protect in place, Americans and others endangered by local turmoil.

In the pre-Civil War period, naval operations involved the enforcement of American law as well as international law and standards. Between the United States ban of the slave trade in 1808 and the onset of the Civil War, American vessels periodically operated against slavers along the coast of West Africa. Carried out in accordance with a treaty with Britain after 1842, operations against the slave trade reflected an "unprecedented sense of Anglo-American cooperation on distant stations" that marked the pre-Civil War period. The American effort never approached the much larger British commitment, which was driven in part by abolition of slavery throughout the British Empire in 1838. Partly because of the US Navy's small size and partly due to its lack of enthusiasm for catching slavers, American commanders seized a total of 24 ships along the coast of Africa, while the British bagged 595. However, as the Civil War approached, the tempo of American naval operations against the slave trade increased. In 1859, the Navy captured five separate carriers of human cargo, including one at the mouth of the Congo River. In 1860, the last full year of peace at home, thirteen slave ships were seized.

In another field of maritime law enforcement, operations against pirates in-cluded landings on Greek islands in 1827 and maritime operations near Hong Kong in the 1850s. The Navy also contributed significantly in the war in Flori-da against the Seminoles in 1835-1842 in which Marines played a land com-bat role.[17] Generally, American naval operations in the pre-Civil War period mirrored those of the much larger British navy, "suppressing piracy, intercepting slaving ships, landing marines, and overawing local potentates from Canton to Zanzibar ..." albeit on a much smaller scale.[18]

American maritime and land operations short of war shared certain charac-teristics. Whether conducted by the Navy in Fiji and Sumatra or the Army in the swamps of south Florida, they usually took place in relatively undeveloped and isolated areas. Operational missions reflected domestic political concerns, whether they involved the freedom of Americans to trade in foreign ports or the rights of citizens to establish farms on the frontier. Opponents were usually small irregular or semi-irregular forces, and operations tended to be diverse and complex, and to lack immediate conclusive results. Additionally, they came in periods of no conventional foreign threat and occurred in places that to Ameri-cans might be considered on the margins, on land in the Indian west and south and at sea in the Caribbean and along Asian coastal regions: Siberia, China, Japan, Korea, the Philippines, and islands in the south Pacific. The Army had the primary job of operating against North American natives, while the Navy handled most of the small engagements outside the nation's territory. In all cases, whether the goal was assertion of commercial and navigation rights or the securing of title to frontier lands, political considerations were central to operational and tactical choices. Success in these operations depended on the interaction of American military forces with local leaders, which in turn required that tactical commanders develop and use political and diplomatic skills, to use Andrew Birtle's phrase, "inherently civil-military in scope."[19]

In the United States, the onset of the Civil War diverted attention from almost all other operational needs; scant attention could be devoted to Indian fights. The Civil War quickly became a conventional war of great size, scope, and duration with cataclysmic social and economic outcomes—the abolition of slavery and devastation of the rebellious states.[20] The war forced the federal government to deal with issues central to interposition and intervention operations in which American forces faced irregular forces. These problems included the legal status of guerilla fighters and hostile populations and the actions taken by military forces in dealing with them. The war also led to massive military involvement in the vast, post-war law enforcement effort, called Reconstruction, "designed to reshape the subject society."[21]

For the Army the period between the Civil War and the war with Spain represented peak involvement in the widest range of gendarme or constabulary operations, with the dominant operational concern the Indian campaigns in the trans-Mississippi West. The Military Division of the Missouri, the geographic subdivision of the Army responsible for the huge territory between the Mississippi River and the Rocky Mountains, published a 95-page list of combat encounters with Indians in 1868-1882.[22] During 1866-1891, clashes with Indians, from frequent minor skirmishes to rare pitched battles, totaled around 1,200.[23] Most of these fights were part of twelve campaigns, but they also included other battles for which soldiers were eligible to receive the Indian Wars Campaign Medal.[24]

As John M. Gates observed, "Much of the army's work on the frontier was that of a frontier constabulary." The Army "served eviction notices on Indians and then forcibly removed them when required." If the tribesmen left the reservations on which they had been placed, the Army "found them and coerced them back," or if necessary fought them until they again surrendered. "Most of the time," according to Gates, "it was routine though difficult police work."[25] For example, Lieutenant John Bigelow, Tenth Cavalry, considered his experience during 1869-1872 at Fort Sill in Indian Territory to have been that of "an army of occupation, to hold the country from which the Indians had been expelled and to keep the Indians within the bounds assigned to them."[26] Likewise, Lieutenant (later Colonel) George Andrews characterized the Twenty-fifth Infantry's ten years in Texas, during 1870-1879, as "a continuous series of building and repairing of military posts, roads and telegraph lines; of escort and guard duty of all descriptions; of marchings and counter-marchings from post to post, and scouting for Indians which resulted in a few unimportant skirmishes."[27] Far from being directed just against the Indians, frontier police work was as likely to involve protection of the reservations, keeping land-hungry settlers off of them as well as keeping Indians on them.

Frequently routine, tedious, and unpleasant, this work was essential to the expansion of the nation. As General William T. Sherman reminded Elizabeth Custer, many years after the death of her husband, "I say that the Indian wars are as much wars as conflicts with foreigners or our own people …. [The] Regular Army of the United States should claim what is true and susceptible of demonstration, that it has been for an hundred years ever the picket line at the front of the great wave of civilization." Sherman's statement reflected a bedrock belief that the Army was the vanguard of an expanding civilization.[28]

Then as now, American soldiers disliked gendarme work and thought that it kept them from concentrating on their proper business of preparing to fight real wars against foreign enemies. Even while the Indian wars were in full swing, "military leaders looked upon Indian warfare as a fleeting bother."[29] This view almost certainly reflected their experience during the Civil War. A Civil War veteran, Brigadier General John Pope, commander of the Department of the Missouri, complained in his annual report of 1881 that Indian campaigning was not "conducive to the proper discharge of military duty or the acquirement, either in theory or practice, by officers or soldiers, of professional knowledge or even of the ordinary tactics of a battalion."[30] Other senior officers shared these views; consequently, the Army never developed a doctrine for Indian warfare, which its officers considered a diversion from the real job of preparing for a big foreign war.[31] Clearly, Pope's comments reflected the widely held view that frontier warfare was "an aberration in a world where the principal menace still lay beyond the sea."[32] Commenting on United States military operations in the 1990s, Richard Shultz reflected on the persistence of such views: "The military defines itself, almost exclusively, as either deterring wars or fighting and winning them. Civil-military operations and those elements of the force structure that engage in them are not judged as being very important—and this has been an enduring aspect of US military culture."[33] Members of think tanks reinforced this inclination by labeling gendarme operations of the 1990s as "missions outside the traditional spectrum of warfighting roles …."[34]

John Pope's generation of officers did not have to look far to find additional grounds for complaining about diversions from preparation for a large foreign war. New operational requirements arose because "the army represented the one federal agency capable of responding to natural disasters with some degree of organization and alacrity."[35]

In the years after the Civil War, the Federal role in society expanded dramatically; there were major responsibilities to be fulfilled for the millions of veterans of the Civil War—cash bonuses, bounty lands, and service pensions to be administered. In addition, the Freedmen's Bureau, intended to ease the transition to freedom for ex-slaves, was moving into "government relief work on a grand scale ... schools, health care, and flood and famine relief to tens of thousands of poor people without regard to their race."[36] The change in the role of government was "immediate, continuous, and dramatic ...," and the mission of the nation's military forces changed as the public sector expanded.[37]

The Freedmen's Bureau, whose full official title was Bureau of Refugees, Freedmen, and Abandoned Lands, operated as an element of the War Department under a Regular officer, Major General Oliver Otis Howard. Military officers provided some of the staff for the bureau, whose primary purpose was "to protect the interests of former slaves."[38] But the Army's main role in the post-Civil War South was enforcement of Federal law, including the supervision of elections. The troop strength in the region declined throughout the period 1865-1876, rapidly at first, from about 200,000 at war's end to under 12,000 by the autumn of 1869, and finally to about 6,000 at the end of Reconstruction in 1876. Overall, Army involvement in Reconstruction was judicious, restrained, and responsible, but it was anathema to southern whites seeking to reassert political control of the formerly secessionist states and the newly free black population. Recently returned to Congress, southern representatives codified their view in the *Posse Comitatus* provision of the War Department Appropriations Act of 1879. This law restricted the use of federal troops to enforce the law within the United States, one of the significant elements of gendarme operations, to cases in which they had explicit Congressional or Constitutional approval.[39] Intended to end Federal efforts against the return of white domination to the South, *Posse Comitatus* succeeded.

Despite the passage of *Posse Comitatus*, Army constabulary operations outside of the South expanded greatly. In the years between 1877 and the end of the century, the Army became involved at least a dozen times in labor disputes and other civil strife. Some of these episodes, such as the occasional range war and efforts to keep impatient homesteaders—"sooners" and "boomers"—off of Indian land until native claims were formally extinguished, were familiar. Other instances, such as the anti-Chinese race riots at Rock Springs, Wyoming, and in Seattle and Tacoma, Washington, during 1885; the nationwide strike of railroad workers against the Pullman Company in 1894; and major work stoppages by the Western Federation of Miners in Idaho during 1892, 1894, and 1899 were problems of the emerging industrial future.[40] At remote forts built to keep the Indians under control, Army officers considered this new prospect and wrote papers about cavalry operations in urban situations and in the protection of industrial property.[41]

In the years after the Civil War, for the first time, the Army responded to a wide range of emergencies. Natural disasters included a grasshopper infestation that ruined farms over a wide swath of the central plains, as well as blizzards, floods, tornadoes, hurricanes, droughts, the devastating San Francisco earthquake and fire of 1906, and other fires, including the great conflagration in Chicago during 1871, as well as the yellow fever epidemics that twice swept through the south in the 1870s.[42] Faced with the Indian wars as the dominant form of combat, and with other operations that rarely required that a shot be fired in anger becoming increasingly significant, military leaders tried "to place the Army on a more enduring basis than afforded by Indian warfare," planning for conventional warfare, and seeking to create an Army that "was designed for the next conventional war rather than the present unconventional war."[43]

After the Civil War, Army forces, especially when engaged against the Indians, rarely operated in groups as large as regiments. During the Pine Ridge campaign of 1890-1891, about 6,000 troops (nearly one fourth of the active force) from all over the West, mobilized by telegraph and transported by rail, converged on the southwestern corner of South Dakota to confront Sioux ghost dancers. Otherwise, only strike-breaking duty brought together forces that were regimental or larger in size. Usually, in the patrolling and skirmishing that took place during the generation after the Civil War, soldiers fought as companies, sometimes as portions of companies, and sometimes in *ad hoc* battalions of two or three companies assembled for a particular campaign. As the twentieth century dawned and the prospect of large-scale foreign conflict emerged, the Army began to train in larger formations—entire regiments, brigades, and even divisions—and to consider seriously the use of such large units.

Meanwhile, through the waning years of the nineteenth century, the Navy continued to be employed in a large number of missions that ranged between interposition and intervention. Piracy remained an occasional problem, but the larger portion of the Navy's effort between the Civil War and the turn of the twentieth century focused on landings in Latin America (thirteen) and in the Pacific (fifteen).[44]

The statement of General Henry H. Shelton, the Chairman of the Joint Chiefs of Staff in the summer of 2000, that "Today the United States strives to keep its military forces combat-ready while, at the same time, engaging in missions that do not routinely involve combat," could have as readily applied to the second half of the nineteenth century as to the beginning of the twenty-first.[45]

Chapter 3
The Twentieth Century

In the first fifty years of the twentieth century, America engaged in three major wars. For most of the period, however, the US military was occupied with operations other than large conventional conflicts. The war against Spain in 1898 distracted the energies of the War and Navy Departments only briefly. As soon as hostilities ended, the United States entered a period in which military operations occurred in familiar regions: in the Caribbean, reflecting the continuing American commitment to the Monroe Doctrine and to the maintenance of stability in Latin America, and in Asian coastal regions facing the United States. Compared to operations in the years between the Civil War and 1898, naval and Marine operations in Latin America grew almost three-fold to thirty-seven in the period between 1899 and 1933; they were, moreover, much longer and more complex than the landings of the earlier period. A substantial land conflict in the Philippines that began in 1898 ended in 1902 with the defeat of a Filipino independence movement. Increasingly, China became a focal point of maritime operations.

Particularly noteworthy was the long duration of some of the Caribbean operations. United States Marines occupied Haiti from 1915 to 1934, and they had units on the other side of the island of Hispaniola, in the Dominican Republic, from 1916 to 1924. For a five-year period, 1926-1930, Marines actively supported the government of Nicaragua against the Sandinista revolution. Major General Smedley Butler, a double Medal of Honor recipient, served in operations in China, Honduras, Panama, Nicaragua, Mexico and Haiti. Another Marine hero, Lewis "Chesty" Puller, was in Haiti from 1919 to 1924 and twice in Nicaragua.[1] "Some of the occupations," as Kenneth Hagan noted, "were quite protracted, and all of them had the objective of altering the political and social structure of the occupied country."[2] These operations were firmly rooted in the operational patterns of the previous century.

Army forces participated in the Army of Cuban Pacification and in management of Cuban government offices between 1906 and 1909 when as many as sixty Army officers served as managers and advisors in law enforcement, public health and sanitation, and other areas. The Army also took part in the occupation of Vera Cruz, Mexico, in 1914, and conducted substantial operations along the Mexican border before and during World War I. After World War I, the

Army permanently replaced the Marine regiment that had garrisoned the Panama Canal Zone with coastal defense and infantry units.[3] In 1933-1934, Colonel Aaron Brown, USA, served as chairman of a tripartite commission that supervised a League of Nations peacekeeping force on the Colombia-Peru border.[4]

Navy forces engaged in humanitarian response operations, disaster relief, and rescue work including the evacuation in 1904 of American citizens in Korea endangered by the war between Russia and Japan, a very early example of a non-combatant evacuation. Sailors landed in Morocco to rescue a kidnapped American in 1904, fought fires and assisted victims of the San Francisco earthquake and fire of 1906, and assisted Greek nationals forced out of Asia Minor by the Turkish government in 1921-1922. The USS *Lexington* even generated almost 4.3 million kilowatt-hours of electricity for Tacoma, Washington, during a month-long emergency in 1930.[5]

Described as gendarme or constabulary operations, these activities usually did not involve combat even against irregular opponents. When they did require armed responses, these gendarme operations differed in key ways from conventional military operations. They almost always involved much lower acceptable levels of firepower in order to stop and apprehend lawbreakers rather than destroy an enemy. Perhaps most important, the military operated under restraints that tolerated only very low levels of ancillary death and destruction. Use of the military in such operations took advantage of their access to supplies and transportation, responsiveness, and commitment to serving the nation. The missions were in response to natural disasters and, less frequently, to "non-natural disasters," ranging from fires to "industrial, transport and miscellaneous accidents."[6]

The military services also became involved in law enforcement, most unpleasantly in the growing number of labor disputes in the waning years of the nineteenth century, protecting the property of large industrial enterprises in confrontations with striking workers. Soldiers hated this duty.[7] Accustomed to seeing themselves as spearheads of civilization as it swept across North America, soldiers found themselves confronting other working class Americans struggling for better wages and working conditions, but the job got done. As Michael Tate observed, "the nineteenth century ended not with images of universally respected cavalrymen dashing across the West in search of renegade Indians and outlaws, but with a growing public dissatisfaction with the army's continued service as a domestic constabulary."[8]

In the nineteenth century, the Army had been involved in "nation-building" activities in two broad categories. One type of activity involved the creation of national infrastructure, and included exploration, surveys, mapping, and construction of roads, water crossings, communications networks, and in the United States massive water-resource projects. Closely related to the first, a second variety concerned scientific inquiries regarding fauna and flora, natural history, geography, geology, and ethnology—studies and assessments that enhanced the ability to understand, exploit, and even conserve the resources of the nation.[9] Its involvement in some aspects of these activities would continue in the twentieth century; however, increasingly other federal, state, and private institutions would occupy center stage in many of these fields.

A third type of nation building, the creation and nurturing of sound public institutions and ultimately a state itself, began at the beginning of the twentieth century beyond the nation's borders. When the United States occupied Cuba, Puerto Rico, and the Philippines after the war with Spain, nation building continued along paths established in the United States, with the creation of the infrastructure on which modern civil society depended—roads, sewer systems, port facilities, and the like. Later, when the occupation of Haiti and the Dominican Republic by the Navy and the Marines involved management of government offices and efforts to create police organizations that were free of corruption, the emphasis moved to the establishment of responsible institutions of government.[10] This drive found its expression in President Woodrow Wilson's declared intent to "teach the South American Republics to elect good men."[11]

At its broadest level, nation building takes on profound significance. As David A. Wilson of RAND Corporation observed in the 1960s, "nation-building" can become "a metaphoric rubric for the social process or processes by which national consciousness appears in certain groups and which, through a more or less institutionalized social structure, act to attain political autonomy for their society."[12] American involvement in this type of nation building reached its peak in the post-war occupations of Japan and Germany. Directed by the American military, the nation building under these occupations aimed at the reform of entire governing structures and the attitudes and values that underlay them. State building in the fullest sense, the occupations were concerted, externally led efforts to replace defeated totalitarian regimes with stable, secure, democratic governments. They were successful.[13]

Recent military involvement in nation building has been much smaller and more sporadic. **Operation Just Cause** in Panama during 1989 was the last twentieth-century operation in which American military forces directed political reconstruction.[14] Two programs sponsored by the American military take a more indirect approach. The International Military Education and Training Program (IMET) strives to assist in nation building in that it exposes foreign officers to American institutions and practices, in the hope that they will be emulated. The post-Cold War Joint Contact Team Program, managed by US European Command and designed to provide advice to the military organizations of former elements and satellites of the Soviet Union, embodies the same impulse.[15]

[15]

However, in the immediate post-Cold War period, nation building fell out of favor with the military and many politicians. Despite recognition that some involvement in public works might be necessary to accomplish humanitarian missions, officers expressed reluctance to become involved in such endeavors. At a conference of Army generals on operations other than war, sponsored by the Army's Training and Doctrine Command in 1995, the soldiers turned their backs on the Army's long history of successful nation-building accomplishments: "participants universally agreed that wide-scale infrastructure refurbishment is not an appropriate task for US military forces."[16] In 1996 Congress restricted military employment in nation building by limiting humanitarian and civic assistance activities associated with military operations to those that used less than $5 million in "equipment, services, and supplies." The same law restricted construction activities to "rudimentary" structures.[17]

When the Cold War became the dominant framework for international relations, the United States armed services entered a period of nearly fifty years in which a large standing force faced a formidable, long-term threat. It was Major General John Pope's dream come true. The American professional military establishment which had been born of the need to police frontiers menaced by Indians and to deal with pirates on the high seas now was required to plan, organize, and operate on a global basis. With its singleness of purpose and "learned habits of restraint," the Cold War provided a prism through which all military operations were viewed, shaped, and evaluated, and it lasted long enough to dominate the experience and attitudes of two generations on both sides of the conflict.[18]

The Cold War capped a process that had been underway since the emergence of the United States as a great power early in the twentieth century. Even before the war with Spain, American military thinkers were looking toward a great power future, studying and reporting on the military institutions of Europe. Organizational reforms at the turn of the century, battleship construction, involvement in a major European war, attempts at joint planning by the Navy and Army, and the development of multiple war plans prior to World War II all centered on preparation for a war with a major power. Increasingly military officers concentrated on plans, roles, organizations, doctrines, and equipment suitable for the armed services of a major power.

During the Cold War this process reached its logical conclusion, as the military came to define itself, "almost exclusively, as either deterring wars or fighting and winning them." Small deployments short of war remained an important aspect of military responsibilities during the Cold War—there were more than two hundred in the period between 1946 and 1975, and more than three hundred for the entire Cold War period—but civil-military operations and those elements of American forces that engaged in them were less important than combat and combat units. This view hardened into what Richard Shultz characterized as "an enduring aspect of US military culture." Concerned primarily with meeting the requirements of major land combat posed by the Cold War confrontation in Central Europe, the Army opposed counterinsurgency missions in Vietnam and elsewhere in the 1960s, and resisted the creation of Special Operations Command and the Office of the Assistant Secretary of Defense for Special Operations and Low Intensity Conflict in the 1980s.[19]

As the Cold War consensus on the role of the armed forces solidified, the classic gendarme functions for which the United States Army was initially established and which played major parts in long periods of the history of the United States Navy were relegated to secondary status.[20] A process took place that resembled developments in the post-World War I British Army.[21] Police duties were insignificant when compared to the large-stakes confrontation of the Cold War.

However, during the Cold War the American military continued to carry out gendarme missions, including deployments within the United States to quell a variety of civil disturbances including the refusals of Southern states to comply with the school desegregation orders of Federal courts. In the autumn of 1962, units of the Army's 82nd and 101st Airborne Infantry Divisions joined federalized Mississippi National Guard troops, Marines, and Air Force elements, a total of 31,000 troops based at a staging area on a Naval Air Station near Memphis, Tennessee. The bulk of these forces, 23,000 in all, then deployed to Oxford, Mississippi, and nearby locations. At Oxford the resistance of white supremacists to the enrollment of a black student, James H. Meredith, for classes at the University of Mississippi, led to widespread violence. On 1 October 1962 Meredith successfully registered for classes, resolving "the greatest constitutional crisis since the Civil War," in which a state's defiance of the orders of the Federal courts and executive branch enforcement of the courts' orders had resulted in widespread violence. Soldiers remained at Oxford through the entire academic year; the last five hundred men did not leave until June 1963.[22]

In the years following the end of World War II, the world was a far from orderly place. Between 1940 and 1966, the demise of the French, British, and Belgian colonial empires spawned fifty-four new, mainly Asian and African, states. By the end of the Cold War, twenty-four additional new countries had made their appearance. By contrast, in the 1990s, seventeen nations emerged from the disintegration of the USSR and Yugoslavia, what Yahya Sadowski called "the Leninist extinction."[23] Moreover, between 1966 and 1989, forty-four wars erupted, some between states and others within states. Nineteen—almost half—continued into the 1990s.[24] Clearly, the same disorder that marked the disappearance of a "world order" anchored by European empires attended the end of the "bipolar world" imposed by the superpower competition.

While American military forces were often engaged in gendarme functions, in the nineteenth century European armies went in a different direction. During the Napoleonic Empire, the French national police or *gendarmerie* was created to carry out a wide range of functions other than waging war against foreign enemies; it was an arm of the Ministry of the Interior, not the French army. Most European states followed the French model, and the new organizations that emerged replaced a host of ad hoc groups. The gendarme forces that replaced these expedient units professionalized and nationalized policing and sometimes constituted more professional military forces than the regular armies they supplemented. Clive Emsley's study of the emergence of national police organizations explains this apparent contradiction: "… the gendarmes were professional soldiers/policemen at a time when the armies of continental Europe were increasingly shifting from a professional mercenary to a conscript base."[25]

The national police forces that emerged from the Napoleonic period conducted many of the same kinds of operations carried out by American regular units in the nineteenth century. They garrisoned barracks in the countryside, patrolled isolated areas, pursued bandits, and helped those whose lives were disrupted by floods, earthquakes, and train wrecks. But the gendarmerie also performed internal security duties more generally associated with European absolutist regimes, gathering intelligence against and tracking the movements of political opponents of the government, collecting taxes, and enforcing conscription.[26] Later in the century, they protected European governments against socialist ideas and labor radicalism. In Europe the gendarmes were important instruments in the consolidation of central state power, while in the United States soldiers carrying out law enforcement duties were transitional figures in the process of transforming territorial governments into states with their own viable law enforcement agencies.[27]

Gendarme or constabulary functions tended to be various and complicated and frequently lacked conclusive, immediate results.[28] Campaigns against bandits or nomadic natives could seem interminable and sometimes very nearly were; they also lacked the focus provided by a big war against a single enemy with a clear outcome. Natural disasters and other catastrophes were rarely predictable and inevitably disrupted established routines. Over long periods, military operations tended to alternate between wars and gendarme operations, but "operations other than war" occupied the armed forces for longer periods of time.[29]

In the post–Cold War period, after nearly fifty years of a relatively static order imposed by the superpower contest, problems demanding swift attention seemed to occur all over the globe and together constituted an operational environment that, when compared to the Cold War, seemed new.[30] American military leaders had a clear and unenthusiastic view of the likely problems posed by involvement in this complex morass.[31] Their political masters "went along with a defense review that argued for a capacity to fight two conventional wars at the same time." This view persisted despite ten years of experience in which only the repetitive pummeling of the Iraqi military and the complex of operations in the Balkans—part bombing, part sanctions enforcement, part peacekeeping, and part humanitarian assistance—bore any resemblance to a major theater war.[32]

During the post-Cold War decade, there was a major gap between the reality of what the armed forces did and what they thought they should legitimately do. Certainly, the vast American experience with small wars and other missions was overlooked. As Robert Utley had noted in 1977 when the Cold War still dominated military reality, "the contribution of the frontier to American military history was of paramount significance, but its contribution to the American military tradition was not of comparable significance."[33] Eliot Cohen characterized the result as a failure to appreciate the long-standing legitimacy and validity of gendarme or constabulary operations, to understand their significance and their demands on resources, and to devote sufficient thought to their proper execution:

> International police work is the wayward child that the Pentagon cannot decide whether to embrace (because it is the only job immediately available and because it justifies the current force structure) or reject (because it conflicts with Cold War concepts of what the military exists to do).[34]

At bottom, an awareness and understanding of the legitimacy of missions has a lot to do with the direction of planning. Peace operations in all of their variations, like many forms of gendarme operations, were very much in the mainstream of things at the end of the 1990s. They were "no longer a makeshift to cope with occasional crises," but "recognized as a core function of the UN [United Nations], and one likely to grow."[35] They were also in a long tradition of American operations. Only when seen through the prism of the Cold War experience were they, as one civilian analyst described them, "unconventional duty."[36]

Chapter 4
Central America and the Caribbean: Panama, Drug Enforcement, and Migrant Interdiction

Military involvement in efforts to reduce the amount of illegal drugs entering the United States goes back at least to 1982, with the establishment of **Operation Bahamas and Turks**, sometimes called "OPBAT." In 1986, President Ronald Reagan labeled drug traffic a threat to national security. Two years later, after debating requiring the armed forces to seal the border with Mexico against drug smugglers, Congress directed the Department of Defense to become involved in detecting and monitoring shipments of illegal drugs and to support law enforcement agencies in preventing drug smuggling.[1]

The rhetorical emphasis on drugs as a threat to national security and even the use of the phrase "war against drugs" did not seem to legitimize the enterprise within the military services that viewed counter-drug operations as outside the normal scope of their duties.[2] **OPBAT**, for example, started as a joint Drug Enforcement Agency and Air Force mission, carried out with United Kingdom and Bahamian agencies, but the Air Force succeeded in ending its involvement in 1986. The Army and the Coast Guard then took over. Despite comparisons to war and allusions to national security, operations aimed at stopping the flow of drugs across the border with Mexico, from the sea on both coasts, and even in producing countries, were bottom law enforcement operations. By placing the armed forces in a lead role in detecting and monitoring the movement of illegal drugs toward the United States, these operations did represent a new form of military cooperation with law enforcement agencies and unfamiliar operational territory.[3] Nevertheless, they all harkened back to law-enforcement operations of earlier peacetime periods, such as enforcement of the nineteenth-century ban on the slave trade and the protection of mail trains by Marines after two such trains were robbed in the early 1920s.[4] The Coast Guard's involvement in the counter-drug efforts also closely resembled that service's contributions to an earlier effort to keep illegal substances out of the United States during the "rum war" of the prohibition era in 1920-1933.[5]

Enforcement of counter-drug policy and curtailing illegal immigration generated considerable work for United States Southern Command was headquartered first in Panama and by the end of the decade in Miami, Florida; that the United States Atlantic Command (Joint Forces Command since October

1999), based in Norfolk, Virginia; and for United States Pacific Command in Hawaii. Counter-drug operations managed by these commands took place largely in the Caribbean, Central America, and the adjacent waters of the Pacific Ocean, historically areas of importance to the United States.

The period from 1989 through 2000 started and ended with American military activity in Panama. Originally code-named **Blue Spoon, Operation Just Cause**, the invasion of Panama, took place in December 1989.[6] Unlike many of the missions undertaken throughout the decade that followed, **Operation Just Cause** was carried out without involving third countries or international organizations. During **Just Cause**, the Panamanian dictator, General Manuel Noriega, was deposed, arrested and brought to the United States to face charges as a drug trafficker.

In the decade that followed **Just Cause**, American activity in Panama remained high, with **Just Cause**[7] followed by a peacekeeping operation known as **Promote Liberty**[8] that lasted from 1990 to 1994, three defense and security operations on anniversaries of **Just Cause** to protect American forces stationed near the Panama Canal (**Diamante 1** in 1994-95; **Diamante 2** in 1995-1996; and **Sustain Liberty** in 1994-1997), and **Safe Haven** in 1994-1995 that was concerned with rescue and detention of Cuban migrants attempting to enter the United States illegally from the sea. At the end of the 1990s, a logistical joint task force, known as **JTF Panama**, supported the withdrawal of American forces from the Canal Zone and the transfer of the Canal to the government of Panama.

Table 1. Operations in Panama, 1989-2000

	Year	Type
Diamante 1	1994-1995	defense/security
Diamante 2	1995-1996	defense/security
JTF Panama	1999-2000	logistics (withdrawal)
Just Cause	1989-1990	offensive (with counter-drug component)
Blue Spoon JTF South Nimrod Dancer		
Promote Liberty	1990-1994	peacekeeping
Backstop Hawk JTF Panama 90 Overwatch		
Safe Haven	1994-1995	immigrant interdiction (Cubans)
Sustain Liberty	1994-1997	defense/security

During the decade, other Caribbean countries, particularly Cuba and Haiti, were of great interest to the United States. American troops had first landed in Cuba in 1898, to expel Cuba's Spanish masters, in "America's first quasi-humanitarian war ...."[9] In the century after 1898, American armed forces carried out long-term interventions in Haiti, the Dominican Republic, and Nicaragua. In the 1990s, the American military, including the Coast Guard, executed a number of operations in the Caribbean, some of which were designed to turn back migrants trying to reach American shores.

The most prominent of these operations was, in large measure, a response to the increasing number of Haitians seeking to leave their island home. Begun in September 1994 and gradually declining in size and importance until it ended six years later, **Operation Uphold Democracy**[10] successfully reinstalled the government of Jean-Bertrand Aristide that had been overthrown by a military junta. In 1994, Haiti faced simultaneous political and economic crises stemming from the junta's seizure of power and the resulting imposition of United Nations sanctions on the military government. Thousands of Haitians tried to leave for the United States, frequently in the most fragile and dangerous vessels. **Uphold Democracy** was meant to "secure our borders," as President William J. Clinton put it, against these waves of illegal immigration as well as to return the legitimate government to power in Haiti.[11]

In addition to **Uphold Democracy**, eleven other operations reflected American concern with illegal immigration from the Caribbean; most focused on Haitian migrants. There were two waves of Haitian migration. The first, in the period from September 1991 to July 1993, stemmed from the political crisis after the Haitian army ousted President Aristide. The second, from October 1993 to September 1994, resulted from a combined political and economic crisis caused by the failure of a negotiated political settlement and the imposition of United Nations sanctions.[12] Sometimes labeled "humanitarian" or "migrant resettlement" operations,[13] all of these deployments focused on keeping illegal immigrants out of the United States.

The George H. W. Bush and Clinton administrations took the same approach to the problem, stopping Haitian vessels outside United States waters in order "to prevent massive numbers from applying for political asylum." The tactic dated from October 1991, when the Bush administration began setting up camps for the Haitians at the American naval base at Guantanamo, Cuba.[14] Originally critical of the Bush approach, Clinton ultimately adopted the same policy.[15]

A sudden flood of Cubans also came during the second wave of Haitian flight that started in the autumn of 1993. Faced with this mass influx, the United States government rescinded a three-year-old policy of automatic asylum for Cubans and directed the Navy and the Coast Guard to apply the same guidelines to those fleeing both Haiti and Cuba.[16] Eight operations between 1991 and 1995 dealt with this problem, underscoring Secretary of Defense William S. Cohen's later insistence that stopping illegal immigration constituted a "critical national interest."[17] Cohen's view would carry over into the administration of President George W. Bush.[18]

Migrant intercept operations involved primarily maritime deployments to pick up people found at sea, and construction, management, and maintenance of detention camps to hold the migrants until their return to their homelands. Navy and Coast Guard vessels and aircraft carried out the offshore patrols. Joint task forces administering the camps included large numbers of Army military police. For example, **Sea Signal** between June 1994 and January 1996 employed an MP brigade headquarters, four battalion headquarters, and fifteen companies, usually deployed in six-month shifts, as well as three security police companies from the Air Force. The camps quickly became overcrowded. Guantanamo soon exceeded its capacity of 15,000 migrants. The United States convinced Panama to allow construction of a camp for as many as 10,000 more, and another camp was built in Suriname.[19] Plans were made for even more facilities in the region, but they were not required. Three of the eleven operations, with facilities planned in Belize, Honduras, and Costa Rica, were never carried out.[20] By the end of the nineties, the flow of migrants abated, and the camps emptied.

Operations involving Cuba responded to other political imperatives, including those created by assertive and politically active, anti-Castro Cuban-Americans centered in Miami. Elements of this community attempted to confront the Cuban government necessitating **Passive Oversight**, a defense and security operation in response to a flotilla organized by a Cuban exile group in July 1997, and **Sentinel Lifeguard**, a show of force after Cuba shot down two aircraft piloted by members of the Cuban-American group "Brothers to the Rescue" in February 1999.

Table 2. Immigrant Interdiction Operations: Cuba and Haiti		
	Cuba/Haiti	Dates
GITMO	both	7 November 1991-1 October 1994
Safe Harbor	Haiti	21 November 1991-1 July 1993
Able Manner	Haiti	13 January-26 November 1993
Sea Signal[1]	both	9 June 1994-18 January 1996
Able Vigil	Cuba	15 August-22 September 1994
Safe Haven[2]	Cuba	27 August 1994-6 March 1995
Deliberate Entry	Cuba	December 1994
Safe Passage[3]	Cuba	1 December 1994-20 February 1995
Distant Haven	Haiti	19 August 1994-20 January 1995
Central Haven Island Haven JTF Belize West Haven		

Table 2. Immigrant Interdiction Operations: Cuba and Haiti (continued)		
	Cuba/Haiti	Dates
Present Haven	both	February 1997

1. The names JTF 160 and Phoenix Perch were also associated with this operation.
2. The names Asilo Seguro and Deliberate Entry were also associated with this operation.
3. The name Phoenix Perch was also associated with this operation.

The use of the name **Safe Haven** unintentionally underscored the dramatic change that had taken place in American attitudes toward immigration. In 1956-1957, the same name had been applied to the rescue and transport to the United States of Hungarians who had fled their country to the West in the chaotic aftermath of the failed revolution of October 1956.[21] In 1994-1995, the name was applied to the movement of Cubans who had tried to enter the United States illegally to camps in Panama prior to repatriating them to Cuba. One **Safe Haven** brought people to the United States to live; another excluded people from entry into the country.

In addition to eight operations concerned with illegal Cuban and Haitian migrants, six operations of the same type focused on illegal Chinese immigration. These operations generally took place in the second half of the decade, while the effort concerning Cubans and Haitians peaked around 1994 and 1995.

Table 3. Immigrant Interdiction Operations: Chinese		
	Region	Year
Marathon Atlantic	Caribbean	1996
Marathon Pacific	South Pacific	1996
Marathon Pacific 99	South Pacific	1999
Present Lift	Caribbean	1997
Prompt Return	South Pacific	1995
Provide Refuge	South Pacific	1993

In the year 2000, Chinese citizens again tried to get into the United States but not in large enough groups for named operations to be established in response. Nevertheless, those who made the attempt were persistent and willing to endure extreme risks and deprivation to succeed. In December 1999, the United States Coast Guard cutter *Munro* intercepted a rusty Chinese freighter, *Wing Fung Lung*, with 4 smugglers and 249 passengers 300 miles off the Pacific coast of Guatemala. In addition to abysmal sanitary conditions and water in the engine room, boarding parties met violent resistance aboard the vessel, the eighteenth such occurrence of the year, compared to only one in 1997. The *Munro's* commander, Captain Wayne Justice, commented that "now you see people who are absolutely determined to reach their destination, and they'll fight back when they realize you are going to stop them."[22]

If the politics of US–Cuban relations gave a special dimension to the problem of illegal immigration, the United States' position regarding refugees from poor countries resembled those taken by other prosperous Western nations. For example, Australian maritime doctrine listed under "constabulary operations" the "prevention of illegal immigration" by the Royal Australian Navy; in 2001 Australia refused entry to a shipload of almost 1,000 Afghan refugees. Nevertheless, Dennis McNamara, Director of International Protections for the UN High Commissioner for Refugees, singled out the US, claiming that the United States "… with a proud history of refugee involvement, has in place some of the most severe restrictions in its history, which affect asylum seekers and refugees trying to enter the United States." McNamara also noted that poorer countries tended to follow the lead of the United States in refugee matters.[23]

The developed nations of the West were not alone in judging people fleeing poor countries as undesirable prospective residents. Rwandan refugees in the mid-1990s were viewed with indifference or outright hostility in neighboring Burundi and Zaire. President Aristide in Haiti and King Hassan in Morocco used the threat of refugee flows in attempts to secure increased aid while prosperous countries gave assistance to curb such movements. In many countries considerable effort went into assuring that the movements of populations were carefully monitored, controlled and even prevented.[24] The International Red Cross, an agency particularly concerned with refugees and their movements, noted that "One country's refugee is another's alien."[25]

During the 1990s, the other major type of law enforcement activities assisted by American forces was counter-drug operations. The use of military force in the "war against drugs" had its origins in laws passed at the end of President Reagan's second term. The Anti-Drug Abuse Act of 1988 authorized military assistance to the anti-narcotics efforts of friendly governments, and the Defense Authorization Act for 1989 made the Department of Defense the lead US government agency "for the detection and monitoring of aerial and maritime transit of illegal drugs into the United States."[26] Overall, the ensuing effort cost well over $10 billion, with US Southern Command spending just over $400 million in Fiscal Year 2000 alone. In the first half of the decade, the US Atlantic Command also had a substantial counter-drug mission, but in October 1995 Southern Command's maritime area of responsibility was expanded to include the Gulf of Mexico, the Caribbean, and portions of the Atlantic Ocean, the major East Coast drug trafficking areas. In addition, US Pacific Command carried out counter-narcotics operations along the Pacific coast of Central America, in Southeast Asia, and in the waters in between.

As an ancillary benefit, the counter-drug program did provide the military useful experience in patrolling, intelligence gathering, and development of skills with advanced technical equipment, such as night vision and communications equipment, for the forces of participating countries.[27] In operations against drug smugglers over the decade, two trends emerged. The number of flying hours and ship days provided by the Department of Defense declined, with the slack taken up by the Coast Guard and Customs Service. At the same time, narcotics traffickers moved gradually from air shipment to water transportation.[28]

The counter-drug mission did not always involve operations with clearly delineated start and end dates. Managed by US Pacific Command, **Wipeout** started in 1990 and continued at least through 1994. This effort, described by the Pacific Command historian as a "multi-agency eradication and enforcement operation, aimed at destroying the marijuana crop in Hawaii, arresting and prosecuting major growers, and discouraging the local populace from pursuing that line of work," involved helicopters from the 25th Infantry Division and the Army National Guard, airplanes from the Air National Guard, and vessels from both the Coast Guard and the Navy.[29] A similar but briefer operation in Jamaica during 1996, called **Weedeater**, eradicated nearly 400,000 marijuana plants, 879 pounds of cured leaf, and 400 pounds of seeds. Carried out by helicopters of the 3rd Infantry Division, **Joint Interagency Task Force East**, and elements of the Marine Corps Reserves, it was truly a joint operation.[30]

Joint Interagency Task Force East was one of three operational joint task forces established in 1989 to control Department of Defense counter-drug operations. It began as **Joint Task Force (JTF) Four** when Congress designated the Department of Defense as the lead agency for detecting and monitoring aerial and maritime drug trafficking and replaced a two-year-old command and control system run by the Customs Service and the Coast Guard. Initially, **JTF Four** reported to United States Atlantic Command. Renamed **Joint Interagency Task Force East** in 1994, it was reassigned to United States Southern Command in 1997. The JTF coordinated operations in the Caribbean and Atlantic from offices in Key West, Florida. **Joint Task Force Five**, organized at the same time and renamed **Joint Interagency Task Force West** in 1994, worked in Pacific waters and reported to United States Pacific Command from its headquarters near San Diego, California. **Joint Task Force Six**, also established in 1989 and stationed in El Paso, Texas, covered the land border with Mexico, working for Forces Command, the Army component of United States Atlantic Command. The activities of all three counter-drug joint task forces involved other government agencies, among them the Drug Enforcement Agency, the Customs Service, the Border Patrol, and the Federal Bureau of Investigation, as well as state and local law enforcement organizations.[31]

Joint Task Force Six's estimates of the number of operations that it conducted were extremely high. The count for the first four years of its existence, through 1993, came to 646, and at the end of the decade it estimated participation in more than 4,300 missions in support of more than 300 law enforcement agencies. These activities included establishment of listening and observation posts and the deployment of electronic sensors as well as more active measures—ground patrols and aerial reconnaissance and transport.[32]

The organizational structure for handling counter-drug operations was unusual, with the three joint interagency task forces managing individual operations of short or indeterminate duration for three different unified commands. No other type of mission was handled in this way, the usual procedure being to set up an individual joint task force reporting to one of the unified commands for each new mission. In the 1990s, at least 44 operations large enough to be included in the annual histories of unified commands were managed by the counter-drug joint task forces or directly by the unified commands. Of the 44 that were identified, 24 took place in Southern Command, 10 in Pacific Command, and 9 in Atlantic Command.[33]

Southern Command, the combatant command most involved in counter-drug operations, and its subordinate, **Joint Interagency Task Force East**, saw beyond the individual operations that proliferated in Central and South America and organized them into six campaigns. The comprehension of the entire effort as a set of campaigns, rather than as a host of disparate operations, dated from the tenure of General Maxwell Thurman, USA, who commanded the 1989 intervention in Panama and understood that the counter-drug effort had to be viewed from an overall regional perspective. Army Generals George Joulwan and Barry McCaffrey retained and refined Thurman's insight. Each campaign subsumed a number of operations in a specific portion of the region. **Carib Ceiling** and **Close Corridor** covered water routes through the Caribbean between the northern coast of South America and Cuba. **Inca Gold** involved land-based operations in South America, and **Central Skies** focused on establishment of a coherent counter-drug operating structure throughout Central America. **Caper Focus** and **Carib Shield** operated on the Pacific and Atlantic coasts of South and Central America, respectively.[34]

Overall, the trend for appropriations for counter-drug operations through the decade was downward, with funding decreasing somewhat faster than the number of operations. Aggregate financial support declined from $1.3 billion at the start of the decade to $975 million per year from 1993 to 1999. As a consequence, Southern Command surveillance, reconnaissance, and intelligence-gathering flights declined, with overall flying hours down 62 percent and the number of days ships spent on patrol also reduced by 62 percent by the end of the period. However, in the same period, the US Customs Service and the Coast Guard increased their counter-drug activities.[35]

Counter-drug and immigrant interdiction operations comprised almost the entire category of military operations concerned with the enforcement of US law. One additional operation conducted by JTF-LA (Los Angeles) related to law enforcement. This 1992 mission supported California law enforcement agencies responding to racial disturbances triggered by the acquittals in the first trial of police officers accused of beating black motorist Rodney King. Military operations in support of the enforcement of US laws, which were classic gendarme or constabulary missions, added up to 60 (or 27 percent) of the 207 total operations counted for 1989-2000.[36]

The counter-drug and immigrant interdiction operations executed beyond the borders of the United States usually took place nearby, particularly in the Caribbean and along the border with Mexico, areas of traditional concern. These locales were the source of real and potential problems, represented in the 1990s by illegal drugs and unwanted immigration, what the Department of Defense's *Quadrennial Defense Review* of 1997 called "transnational dangers."[37] United States operations concerning drugs and unwanted immigrants in areas close to the United States could be said to respond to what Benjamin Miller called "an extrinsic interest," an interest that is based on "the geographical proximity of the region in question to the hegemon or to its most important allies." According to Miller, "proximity to the great power or to its most vital allies makes even a region poor in resources more important than it would have been if located far away."[38] Or, as President James Monroe put it in the portion of his December 1823 message that became known as the Monroe Doctrine, "With the movements in this Hemisphere we are of necessity more immediately connected, and by causes which must be obvious to all enlightened and impartial observers."

Chapter 5
Humanitarian Operations

As far back as the 1870s, when the Army responded to the needs of civilian communities struck by epidemics and insect infestations, humanitarian operations had been a part of the work of US armed forces. In the post-Cold War decade, Department of Defense (DOD) efforts to provide humanitarian assistance and disaster relief depended on requests from affected countries and were guided by assessments by the American embassy at the scene and the resources available. The State Department's Office of Foreign Disaster Assistance (OFDA) served as the main coordinating agency. Other assistance programs involving DOD agencies included donation of excess property, use of space-available transportation for supplies donated by non-governmental agencies, and limited assistance for restoration of facilities, utilities, and other infrastructure.[1]

Humanitarian missions from 1990 to 2000 totaled 61. Among them were non-combatant evacuations and other rescues, and 28 responses to natural disasters caused by weather, mainly floods, and by earthquakes.[2]

Fifteen of the responses were carried out in the Western Hemisphere, seven in North America and eight in Central America and the Caribbean. But there were responses to natural disasters in all parts of the world—Asia (four), Europe (three), Africa (two), and the South Pacific (six). Averaging nearly three responses every year, US military humanitarian assistance missions reacted to only a very small portion of the 2,468 natural disasters listed for the period by the Red Cross and Red Crescent.[3] Table 4, "Responses to Natural Disasters," shows the geographic distribution and the variety of types of the 31 disasters to which American forces responded.

Table 4. Responses to Natural Disasters			
Name	Region	Type	Duration
Antigua 90 Hurricane Hugo	Caribbean	hurricane	1990
Atlas Response Silent Promise	Africa	flood	2000
Avid Response I and II	Europe	earthquake	1999
Balm Restore	South Pacific	cyclone	1992-93
Caribbean Castle	Caribbean	hurricane	1999

Table 4. Responses to Natural Disasters (continued)

Name	Region	Type	Duration
Caribbean Express	Caribbean	hurricane	1995
Colombia 94	South America	earthquake	1994
Disaster Relief JTF Hurricane Georges	Caribbean	hurricane	1998
Fiery Vigil JTF Marianas 91	Southeast Asia	Rescue/evacuation temporary shelter	1991
Fundamental Relief Full Provider	Caribbean/North America	hurricane	1998
Fundamental Response	South America	floods	1999-2000
Hot Rock	Europe	volcano	1992
Hurricane Floyd	North America	hurricane	1999
India 2001	South Asia	earthquake	2001
JTF Aguila (Eagle)	Central America	hurricane	1998
JTF Andrew	North America/ Caribbean	hurricane	1992
JTF Hawaii Garden Isle	South Pacific	typhoon	1992
JTF Marianas 92	South Pacific	typhoon	1992
Noble Response	Sub-Sahara	floods	1998
Philippines 90	Southeast Asia	earthquake	1990
Recuperation	North America	winter storms	1998
Sea Angel Productive Effort	South Asia	cyclone/typhoon	1991-92
Strong Support Fuerte Apoyo JTF Bravo	Central America	hurricane	1998-99
Tunisia	Africa	storm	1990
Typhoon Mike	Southeast Asia	typhoon	1990
Typhoon Ofa	South Pacific	typhoon	1990
Typhoon Val	South Pacific	typhoon	1991-92
Water Pitcher	South Pacific	drought	1992
Western Fires 1994	North America	wild fires	1994
Western Fires 1996	North America	wild fires	1996
Western Fires 2000 Lumberjack Thunder	North America	wild fires	2000

In three of these operations, elements of the Department of Defense came under the simultaneous direction of two separate Federal agencies, the Federal Emergency Management Agency (FEMA) for the territory of the United States and the State Department's Office of Foreign Disaster Assistance for emergency aid elsewhere. The first of these operations was the response to the damage done by Typhoon Ofa in Samoa. In independent Western Samoa, OFDA managed United States relief operations, while in American Samoa FEMA took charge; military support on both sides of the island came from United States Pacific Command. The same arrangement obtained on Samoa during **Operation Balm Restore** in December 1992, after a tropical cyclone hit the island. In the Caribbean six years later, after Hurricane Georges swept through the region, the United States Southern Command worked for the same two agencies in providing assistance in Puerto Rico and in the Dominican Republic.

Disaster relief operations sometimes made use of annual training for Reserve Component units. This was especially true in Central America, where a large number of short-term engineer missions under the control of **Joint Task Force Bravo** labored to restore local infrastructure damaged by hurricanes. Reserve units rotated through Nicaragua and Honduras on two-week tours of active duty for training. Starting in the 1980s, the practice continued through the 1990s, and accelerated at the end of the decade in the wake of the devastation caused by Hurricane Mitch in Central America. For example, elements of Wisconsin Army National Guard units—the 724th Engineer Battalion, the 106th Quarry Team, and the 829th Engineer Detachment—with active component engineers from the Army and the Marines built educational and medical facilities in Nicaragua during the summer of 2000 as part of **Joint Task Force Sebaco**, a fifteen-day training rotation for the Guardsmen. Their work was part of a continuing effort to restore infrastructure ruined by Hurricane Mitch and involved annual training for about six thousand Army Reserve Component soldiers, with about five hundred of them in Central America at any given time.[4]

During the 1990s, humanitarian operations included eighteen non-combatant evacuation operations (NEOs). These operations were firmly rooted in the two-hundred-year tradition of naval responses to the distress of American citizens in foreign countries. However, in earlier times, United States forces, usually the Navy and Marines, had directed their efforts at protecting American nationals in place rather than quickly removing them from tense and dangerous situations.[5] Evacuations in the nineties involved Navy Amphibious Ready Groups and Marine Expeditionary Units as well as special operations forces and aircraft.

The 22nd Marine Expeditionary Unit (**Special Operations Capable**) in US European Command was frequently employed in these operations both in Africa and Europe. In 1996, the unit was involved in two nearly simultaneous

African evacuations, in Liberia (**Assured Response**) and the Central African Republic (**Quick Response**). In addition, the 22nd was alerted for at least two more NEOs during 1997-1998, **Autumn Shield** in Albania and **Guardian Retrieval** in Zaire. In the spring of 1997, after two months on alert for **Guardian Retrieval**, the 22nd went directly into Freetown, the capital of Sierra Leone, for **Noble Obelisk**, carrying out three evacuations within five days "in the midst of near anarchy."[6]

Table 5. Completed Noncombatant Evacuations		
Name	Country	Year
Assured Response	Liberia	1996
Distant Runner	Rwanda	1994
Eastern Exit	Somalia	1991
Firm Response	Congo (Brazzaville)	1997
Kuwait 98	Kuwait	1998
Liberia 94	Liberia	1994
Noble Obelisk	Sierra Leone	1997
Quick Lift 1991	Zaire	1991
Quick Response	Central Africa	1996
Romania 89	Romania	1989
Safe Departure	Eritrea	1998
Sharp Edge	Liberia	1990-91
Silver Anvil	Sierra Leone	1992
Silver Compass JTF Liberia	Liberia	1992
Silver Fox	Tajikistan	1992
Silver Wake	Albania	1997
Sudan 91	Sudan	1991
Yemen	Yemen	1994

In terms of effort and resources, the eighteen evacuations do not represent the whole story of noncombatant rescues. Fifteen other NEOs were planned; fourteen were cancelled as situations appeared to stabilize. The fifteenth, **JTF NEO**, was a standing plan for evacuation of military dependents and other noncombatants from Korea in case of war. Of the thirty-three noncombatant evacuations that were either executed or planned, eleven came during the four-year Bush presidency and twenty-two during the eight Clinton years, so the level of this activity throughout the 1990s remained generally constant.

Like those that were completed, noncombatant evacuations which were planned but not executed tended to center on sub-Saharan Africa. All but one of the operations that were planned but not executed came in the three years from 1997 through 1999. Nine involved African countries. Overall, twenty-two of the thirty-three total and thirteen of the eighteen that were actually implemented took place in the sub-Saharan region, with four carried out and another planned in Liberia alone. The large number of these operations in Africa reflected a period of conflict and instability in the sub-Saharan region with its forty-six countries and immense internal differences in culture and language.[7] A *New York Times* editorial writer called the situation a "chain of interconnected conflicts that are ravaging a vast swath of Africa from the Horn of Africa to Namibia."[8] The recurring need to assist the many victims of these conflicts underscored the relationship between war and humanitarian operations. One created the need for the other, prompting *New York Times* Nairobi bureau chief Ian Fisher to observe that "humanitarianism is, at its core, about war …."[9] The concentration of evacuation operations, planned and executed, in Africa meant that most of the burden of planning and controlling these operations fell on United States European Command headquartered in Stuttgart, Germany.[10]

Planning for possible evacuations reflected the experience of carrying out such operations as well as a new emphasis on Africa in American policy in the 1990s. President Clinton made two trips to the continent, one to East Africa in the spring of 1998, called **Eagle Vista**, and another to Nigeria two years later.[11] Nineteen more operations, among them major ones such as **Restore Hope** in Somalia, **Support Hope** in Rwanda and Zaire, and **Atlas Response** in Mozambique, took place on the continent.[12] The missions ranged from delivery of food to famine-stricken areas of Kenya and Tanzania to logistical support for stability operations in Angola 1992 and Sierra Leone in 2000, and included the **Incident Reach** missile strikes in Sudan and Afghanistan during August 1998, in retaliation for the bombing of the American embassies in Kenya and Tanzania, an operation that one observer termed "modern-day gunboat diplomacy by airpower."[13] At the end of the decade, the Agency for International Development called the Horn of Africa the United States government's "highest-priority humanitarian emergency in the world currently."[14] The increased number of operations in Africa reflected this concern as well as the instability that marked the region in the 1990s.

The need to plan for non-combatant evacuations in advance went beyond concerns about Africa and mirrored the sheer increase in the number of American embassies. By the end of the 1990s there were 260 embassies around the world, some in new and unstable countries. Moreover, each embassy constituted a potential target for terrorism and was, therefore, a candidate for evacuation planning.[15]

Table 6. Noncombatant Evacuations Planned but not Executed		
Name	Country	Year
Autumn Shelter	Dem. Repub. of Congo	1998
Balkan Calm II	Albania	1999
Bevel Edge	Cambodia	1997
Bevel Incline	Indonesia	1998
Distant Rescue	Burundi	1995
Guardian Retrieval	Zaire	1997
Joint Guarantor	Bosnia	1999
JTF NEO	Korea	(since) 1998
JTF Sarajevo	Bosnia	1992
Shadow Express	Liberia	1998
Shepherd Venture	Guinea-Bissau	1998
Silent Guide	Ivory Coast	1999
Silver Guardian	Angola	1992
Silver Knight	Albania	1998
Autumn Shield		
Victor Squared	Haiti	1991
	Eritrea	1999
	Ethiopia	1999

The entire group of humanitarian operations, including rescue, evacuation, and disaster relief operations, represented a significant portion of the overall operational activity of the American military in the 1990s. Other humanitarian efforts included training and assistance in clearing land mines in Afghanistan and in Central America—Operations **Clean Sweep** in 1995-1996 and **Safe Passage 88** in 1988-1991, provision of medical supplies in various parts of the former Soviet Union in **Operation Provide Hope** during 1992-1994, and several efforts to aid people displaced by war and famine. Also included was one operation to provide assistance in the development of viable government institutions. From 1993 to 1997, this was the task of the Haiti Assistance Group working in conjunction with **Operation Uphold Democracy** and its United Nations successors.

The United Nations operation that supplanted **Uphold Democracy** in March 1995, known as the **United Nations Mission in Haiti** or **UNMIH**, brought US forces, mainly from the 25th Infantry Division, under UN command. However, Major General Joseph Kinzer, USA, Deputy Commander of Fifth US Army, served as both the UN commander and the commander of the American forces. On 4 June 1995, the Second Cavalry Regiment replaced the 25th Infantry in Haiti. Through the rest of the year and into early 1996, the forces participating in the operation were gradually reduced until the UN mandate expired on 29 February 1996. By the spring of that year, only a small American training cadre remained.[16]

Two of the decade's humanitarian missions responded to terrorist events. **Resolute Response** followed the bombing of American embassies in Kenya and Tanzania in 1998, and **Determined Response** came after the attack on the USS *Cole* while it was anchored in the Yemeni port of Aden in October 2000. Overall, humanitarian operations totaled to 61 (or 29 percent) of the 207 operations in the period.

The American military was not the only organization that faced what appeared to be an accelerating operational tempo. In the first half of the 1990s, the United Nations High Commissioner for Refugees dealt with increasing numbers of displaced people fleeing for their lives or seeking better opportunities for themselves and their families. Worldwide in 1992, there were 83 million people who had emigrated from one country and settled in another. There were 15 million economic migrants in Western Europe and about the same number in North America, where the United States absorbed about two million legal and illegal immigrants per year. While there had been 22 million refugees and displaced people in 1985, ten years later the number was 37 million.[17] Other humanitarian organizations including the International Red Cross and Red Crescent Movement and the World Food Program also spent more of their time and money on refugees and populations displaced by war.[18] In Rwanda in 1994 more than one hundred such groups were at work, providing food, medical care, housing, transportation, and education.[19]

For military organizations involved in relief efforts, the presence of large numbers of private charities represented substantial coordination challenges, usually addressed through the establishment of civil-military operations centers or more directly focused humanitarian operations centers.[20] The need for a systematic approach to coordination became clear during the operation in Somalia, where the first Civil Military Operation Center (CMOC) was established in December 1992. The US command, along with liaison officers from other members of the multinational force, used the CMOC to coordinate military support for convoys of relief supplies, to assign pier space for supplies arriving in Mogadishu, and to arrange port access. Ultimately nine CMOCs were established in Southern Somalia, one for each humanitarian relief sector. Before the operation ended, the Civil Military Operations Center controlled issue of identification cards, tracked the movement of relief supplies, and worked closely with the United Nations' Humanitarian Operations Center (run by the UN), creating a focal point for all relief agencies in country.[21]

Table 7. Non-governmental Organizations Operating in Rwanda and Neighboring Countries (Summer/Autumn 1994)

Organization	Specialty
*Action Aid/Assist	equipment
*Action Internationale Contre la Faim/France	emergency medical care
*Action Internationale Contre la Faim/USA	emergency medical care
*Action Nord Sud	distribution of seeds and tools, livestock vaccination
*Adventist Development and Relief Agency	medical, shelter, food
*African Medical and Research Foundation	health care
*Africare	sanitation services
Air Serv International	humanitarian flights
American Jewish Joint Distribution Committee	food, health
American Jewish World Service	emergency medical care
*American Refugee Committee	health care
American Red Cross	
Baptist World Aid	
Baptist World Alliance	
Brother's Brother Foundation	medical supplies and equipment
Canadian Baptist Missionaries	
*CARE International	camp management, distribution and monitoring, food, sanitation, seeds and tools
*Catholic Relief Services	food, other assistance
Christian Children's Fund	health
*Christian Reformed World Relief Committee	seeds and tools
Church World Action-Rwanda	coalition
Direct Relief International	health
Doctors of the World	
Doctors without Borders, USA, Inc.	
*Feed the Children/Europe	food, emergency supplies
Food for the Hungry International	
International Aid Inc.	health
*International Committee, Red Cross	
International Federation of Red Cross and Red Crescent Societies	
*International Medical Corps	health care
*International Rescue Committee	sanitation
Jesuit Refugee Service/USA	
Lutheran World Federation	camp management, distribution monitoring
MAP International	health

Table 7. Non-governmental Organizations Operating in Rwanda and Neighboring Countries (Summer/Autumn 1994) (continued)

Organization	Specialty
*Medicins Sans Frontieres/France	water, sanitation
Mercy Corps International	health
Operation USA	medicines
Oxfam America	airlift, money
Refugees International	
Salvation Army	
*Samaritan's Purse	health
Save the Children (USA)	
*Save the Children's Fund/UK	non-food aid, health
*Solidarites	logistical support
Unitarian Universalist Service Committee	
United Methodist Committee on Relief	
World Concern	supplies, medicines
*World Food Program	
*World Relief	medical
*World Vision Relief and Development	non-food items, sanitation, seeds, tools
YMCA of the USA	

Source: InterAction, "Rwanda Crisis Situation Report No. 10 Draft," 20 October 1994; US Agency for International Development, Bureau for Humanitarian Response, Office of US Foreign Disaster Assistance (OFDA), "Rwanda—Civil Strife/Displaced Persons Situation Report #1 Fiscal Year (FY) 1995."

Note: As of October 1994, there were 118 NGOs operating in Rwanda according to the US Agency for International Development situation report, 17 October, 1994.

* Direct recipient of US government funding as reported by the US Agency for International Development; others may have received such support indirectly from international organizations such as the United Nations High Commissioner for Refugees and the United Nations Children's Fund.

The year 1992 saw an exceptional number of humanitarian operations. Stephen Guerra's observation that for the US Navy "1992 stands out as the year with the greatest number of such efforts" applied to the entire defense establishment.[22] During the year, the American military either responded to or continued work from the preceding year on seven natural disasters, four in the South Pacific, one in Europe, one in South Asia, and one—Hurricane Andrew—in North America and the Caribbean.

Joint Task Force Andrew, the military response from August to October 1992 to the hurricane of the same name, illustrated the types of military units that were in high demand for such operations. The force included eight Army Military Police companies among the 106 deploying units representing all services. In addition there were a press camp headquarters detachment (public affairs) and 15 medical units, among them air ambulance, entomology, and public health personnel. Nineteen deploying units, almost one out of every five, were either Navy or Army engineers; they included combat and construction units, a bridge-building company, firefighters, and divers.[23] With the military providing this wide range of services—medical care, law enforcement, and engineering—at no cost to state and local governments, it was difficult to withdraw units from domestic disaster relief missions such as **JTF Andrew**.[24]

In addition to **Joint Task Force Andrew**, activities in 1992 included three non-combatant evacuations, conducted in Sierra Leone, Liberia, and Tajikistan, with two others planned for Bosnia and Angola. Three other humanitarian missions—**Fiery Vigil** in the Philippines, **Provide Hope** in the former Soviet Union, and **Provide Relief** in Somalia—also required planning and operational support. There were sanctions enforcement missions and a humanitarian assignment in the Balkans, and **Operations Southern Watch**, **Northern Watch**, and **Provide Comfort** were all active in Southwest Asia. At the same time, the active-duty force continued to decline in strength. It was gradually being reduced from its 1980s level of just over two million and now stood at 1.8 million.[25] If there was a year in which the operational tempo seemed nearly overwhelming, it was 1992.

In general, this kind of humanitarian operation fit squarely within the nineteenth century tradition of gendarme operations. As Clive Emsley wrote in his study of the various European gendarmerie during the nineteenth century, "assisting the population in times of accident or natural disaster was a way of promoting the state as a guardian of its citizens ...," so they fought fires and assisted with rescue and recovery after floods, earthquakes, volcanoes, explosions, and train crashes.[26] The big difference involved the size of the stage on which such work was carried out. In nineteenth century Europe, the gendarmerie acted within national borders, promoting and asserting the primacy of the state while providing useful services to the citizenry in troubled times, just as United States forces had done, carrying out similar functions in the same period, mainly in the trans-Mississippi West. In the post-Cold War world, United States forces acted on an international scale bringing assistance to desperate people, sometimes in concert with other nations and sometimes under the aegis of the United Nations or the North Atlantic Treaty Organization. While the worldwide scope of operations and the frequent participation in international efforts set American operations after the Cold War apart from earlier gendarme operations elsewhere, the type of mission itself was far from new.

Table 8. Humanitarian Operations Worldwide			
Name	**Region**	**Type**	**Duration**
Clean Sweep	Central America	humanitarian (de-mining)	1995-96
Determined Response	SW Asia	explosion	2000
Guardian Assistance	Sub-Sahara	humanitarian (assist refugees)	1996
Haiti Assistance Group	Caribbean	nation-building	1994-97
High Flight	Sub-Sahara	rescue (airplane crash)	1997
Phoenix Lion			
Mongolia	Central Asia	humanitarian	1991-95
Noble Response	Sub-Sahara	humanitarian	1998
Persistent Support	North America	humanitarian	1998
Provide Hope	CIS	humanitarian	1992-98
Provide Relief	Sub-Sahara	humanitarian (UN peace enforce)	1992-93
Resolute Response	Sub-Sahara	humanitarian	1998
Safe Passage 88	South Asia	humanitarian (de-mining)	1988-91
Support Hope	Sub-Sahara	humanitarian	1994
Provide Assistance			
Quiet Resolve			
Turquoise			
UNAMIR			

Note: Operations listed as Non-combatant Evacuations, responses to natural disasters, and operations in the Balkans and concerning the Saddam Hussein regime in Iraq are listed separately.

Chapter 6
Stability Operations

Except in Panama, United States involvement in stability operations during the period took place in a multinational framework, with other participant nations, with some kind of international mandate, and alongside numerous non-governmental organizations.[1] Operations that involved enforcement of international law and standards, as asserted by United Nations Security Council resolutions, or in concert with North Atlantic Treaty Organization allies, formed the bulk of the missions. Others came at the request of nations embroiled in disputes or from regional groups in need of assistance.

Except for their complexity and global distribution, stability operations resembled classic gendarme operations. Participating federal agencies included the State Department, the Department of Defense, the Central Intelligence Agency, the National Security Council and the Departments of Justice, Treasury, and Transportation, among others. Participation by non-governmental organizations grew to the point where more than one hundred such entities took part in relief work in Rwanda.[2] The need to keep the participants from getting in each other's way complicated operations and became an operational requirement. Even the missions that involved or included combat operations also required establishment and enforcement of law and order, and fell within the framework stated by the 1997 *Quadrennial Defense Review*: "US forces encourage adherence to the international norms and regimes that help provide the foundation for peace and stability around the globe ...."[3]

Like humanitarian operations and missions related to the enforcement of United States law, stability operations formed a large portion of the decade's effort, totaling 50 (or 24 percent) of 207 operations; as the decade ended there was no reason to expect that they would decline in complexity or in number.[4] Stability operations involving American forces clustered in two distinct and substantial groups, one concerning the Balkans (Table 9) and another focused on operations against the regime of Saddam Hussein in Iraq (Table 13). A handful of operations stood outside these two groupings (Table 14).

Table 9. Unclassified Names of American Operations Involved in the Enforcement of International Law and Standards in the Balkans, 1992-2001

Name	Type	Duration	Authority
Able Sentry	peacekeeping	1993-99	UN/under NATO 1999
Auger Express	reconnaissance (peacekeeping)	1998	NATO
Autumn Shield	defense/security	1998	
Balkan Calm	peace observers	1998	NATO
Deliberate Falcon	show of force	1998	NATO
Deliberate Force	air strike	1995	NATO
Deny Flight	sanctions enf	1993-95	NATO/UN

Balkan Shield
  Nomad Vigil
  Persuasive Force			

Determined Falcon	show of force	1998	NATO
Determined Force	air strike	1995	NATO
Determined Forge	sanctions enf(sea)	1998-99	NATO
Eagle Eye	peacekeeping	1998-99	NATO
Joint Guarantor Determined Guarantor			
Essential Harvest	peacekeeping	2001	NATO
Joint Endeavor	peacekeeping	1995-96	NATO
Decisive Edge	sanctions enf(air)	1995-96	NATO
Decisive Endeavor			
Decisive Enhancement	sanctions enf(Sea)	1995-96	NATO
Quick Lift 1995	logistics		
Joint Forge	peacekeeping	1998-99	NATO
Decisive Forge	peacekeeping	1998-99	NATO
Deliberate Forge	sanctions enf(air)	1998-99	NATO
Joint Guard	peacekeeping	1996-98	NATO
Decisive Guard	peacekeeping	1996-98	NATO
Deliberate Guard	sanctions enf(air)	1996-98	NATO
Determined Guard			
Nomad Endeavor	logistics	1996	
Joint Guardian	peacekeeping	1999-	UN
Decisive Guardian	peacekeeping	1999-	UN
Maritime Guard	sanctions enf(sea)	1992-93	UN
Maritime Monitor	sanctions enf(sea)	1992	UN

Table 9. Unclassified Names of American Operations Involved in the Enforcement of International Law and Standards in the Balkans, 1992-2001 (continued)

Name	Type	Duration	Authority
Noble Anvil	air strikes	1999	NATO

Allied Force
  Flexible Anvil
  Nimble Lion
  Sky Anvil			

Provide Promise	humanitarian	1992-96	
Provide Refuge 1999	humanitarian	1999	
Sharp Fence	sanctions enf(sea)	1993-95	UN
Sharp Guard	sanctions enf(air)	1993-95	UN
Sharp Vigilance	sanctions enf(air)	1992-93	UN/NATO
Shining Hope	humanitarian (displaced people)	1999	NATO
Allied Harbour Sustain Hope			
Sky Monitor		1992	

The United Nations, under whose aegis parts of the effort in the Balkans took place, was not exactly a paragon of denominative clarity. The international organization put ten separate names on its post–Cold War operations in the Balkans and added a bewildering array of acronyms. However, the United Nations did not adopt the American practice of frequently changing the names of ongoing operations.

Table 10. United Nations Peace Operations in the Balkans, 1992-2000

	Location	Dates
UN Protective Force (UNPROFOR)	B&H, Croatia, FRY, Macedonia	Feb 92-Mar 95
UN Peace Forces (UNPF)		Mar 95- Jan 96
UN Protective Force (UNPROFOR)	B&H	Mar- Dec 95
UN Confidence Restoration Operation in Croatia (UNCRO)	Croatia	Mar 95- Dec 96
UN Preventive Deployment Force (UNPREDEP)	Macedonia	Mar 95- Feb 99
UN Mission in Bosnia & Herzegovina (UNMIBH)	B&H	Dec 95-
UN Transitional Administration for Eastern Slavonia, Baranja, and Western Sirmium (UNTAES)	Croatia	Jan 96-Jan 98
UN Civil Police Support Group (UNPSG)	Croatia	Jan-Oct 98
UN Mission of Observers in Prevlaka (UNMOP)	Croatia	Jan 96-
UN Interim Administration in Kosovo (UNMIK)	Kosovo	Jun 99-

The diversity of the operations in the Balkans went beyond overlapping, repetitive, and confusing names and an apparently large variety of purposes. Sometimes, individual units participated simultaneously in combat action as well as humanitarian relief, a combination known as "cops and docs." The 26th Marine Expeditionary Unit, which began a six-month deployment to the Balkans at the end of April 1999, participated in both **Noble Anvil**, the bombing of Serbia, and **Shining Hope**, the provision of supplies to refugees from Kosovo in Albanian camps. In June, when the bombing campaign ended, 2,200 Marines of the 26th went to Macedonia as peacekeepers, under **Operation Joint Guardian**, where they stayed for a month. Six weeks later, the 26th was in Turkey on a humanitarian mission, **Avid Response**, in the wake of an earthquake.[5]

For all of their apparent diversity, operations in the Balkans constituted parts of a single prolonged effort to bring peace and stability to the region. For the 1990s, this cluster of missions was the nearest equivalent to the "major theater war" envisioned by American military planners. The effort involved all types of American forces in conjunction with the forces of friendly nations, cost billions of dollars, and went on for the entire decade. It did not meet the definition of major theater war set by the 1997 *Quadrennial Defense Review*, as taking place at the "high end of the crisis continuum," nor did it resemble a conventional war or cause a large number of US casualties.[6] The *Quadrennial Defense Review* was silent on the exact size and nature of the force needed to respond to a major theater war, but its authors clearly had in mind a large commitment of forces, probably based on "the Gulf War case—envisioning the deployment of a massive, armor-heavy force supported by a vast fleet and hundreds or thousands of aircraft ...."[7]

Operations in the Balkans had some of the attributes of a response to a large crisis, using as much as 40 percent of the Air Force's combat aircraft.[8] In any case, as an Institute for Defense Analyses study observed, "More and more, humanitarian assistance, peace operations, and other military operations other than war (MOOTW) have become the norm."[9] While a major theater war was not likely, "major and persistent situations," as a Center for Naval Analyses writer referred to the Balkans, Iraq, Haiti, and Somalia, became prominent parts of the international landscape.[10] These groups of operations could be seen as "mini-containment clusters," including "everything from strikes and shows of force down to humanitarian assistance and nation-building."[11]

In 1999, when the Office of the Secretary of Defense (OSD) reported to Congress on the number of operations underway in the decade, it listed thirteen separate operations in the Balkans as "major smaller scale contingencies," rather than noting a single overall enterprise to which all of the operations were connected. The OSD list reflected the tendency to assign new names to iterations or elements of single tasks in the Balkans. For example, **Joint Endeavor** (December 1995-December 1996), **Joint Guard** (December 1996-June 1998),

Joint Forge (June 1998-June 1999), and **Joint Guardian** (June 1999-) all designated different periods of what was essentially a single, long-term Balkan peacekeeping operation. The OSD report cemented the impression of numerous organizations at work in a complicated situation and did nothing to dispel difficulties in understanding and tracking the operations. Moreover, by organizing them by year and by type rather than by locale and by singling out operations that were components of other operations, the report obscured the interconnected nature of these efforts and their common purpose.[12]

Table 11. The OSD Balkan Thirteen		
Name	Nature	Period
Deliberate Force	Air strikes	Aug-Sep 95
Deliberate Guard	Air support for Joint Guard	Dec 96-Jun 98
Deny Flight	Sanctions enforcement	Apr 93-Dec 95
Maritime Monitor	Sanctions enforcement	Jul-Nov 92
Maritime Guard (follow-on to Maritime Monitor)	Sanctions enforcement	Dec 92-Jun 93
Sharp Guard (follow-on to Maritime Guard)	Sanctions enforcement	Jun 93-Dec 95
Decisive Enhancement (Support of Joint Endeavor)	Sanctions enforcement	Dec 95-Dec 96
Able Sentry	Peacekeeping	Jun 93-Feb 99
Joint Endeavor	Peacekeeping	Dec 95-Dec 96
Joint Guard (follow-on to Joint Endeavor)	Peacekeeping	Dec 96-Jun 98
Joint Forge (follow-on to Joint Guard)	Peacekeeping	Jun 98-Jun 99
Eagle Eye	Air verification of cease fire	Oct 98-Mar 99
Provide Promise	Humanitarian	Jul 92-Jan 96

Multiple joint task forces operating in the Balkans carried out different pieces of what could have been characterized as a single overall campaign. Whether keeping the peace, delivering food and medicine, enforcing sanctions, or dropping bombs, these forces accomplished their missions simultaneously or nearly so and in the same small region, albeit under different operational names. These operations involved 6,149 personnel in 1994, 17,221 two years later, and declined to 8,650 at the end of 2001.

While their different missions as peacekeepers, providers of humanitarian assistance, or enforcers suggested distinctions and separation, the operations came together on the ground as parts of the overall effort to stabilize the small portion of southeastern Europe known as "the Balkans." As parts of the American contribution to United Nations and North Atlantic Treaty Organization efforts, these operations also came together at the headquarters of the Southern Europe Task Force at Aviano, Italy, or at the United States European Com-

mand Headquarters at Patch Barracks in Stuttgart, Germany. As components
of multinational operations, they came together with the forces of other nations
in the NATO Headquarters at Mons, Belgium.

One United States government agency did view the operations in the Balkans as a unified entity. In computing the costs of operations in the Balkans, the
General Accounting Office (GAO) considered all of the efforts to be of a single
piece. The total of funds specifically allocated for the un-programmed missions
known as contingency operations and spent in the region from 1992 to 2000
came to $13.82 billion or 62 percent of the Defense outlay for contingency
operations of almost $21.3 billion.[13]

Table 12. DOD and US Government Costs (in millions) for Support Operations, 1992-1995

	DOD	Total
Somalia	$ 1,522.1	$ 2,223.1
Former Yugoslavia	784.0	2,186.9
Rwanda	144.1	573.7
Haiti	953.9	1,616.7

Source: US General Accounting Office, *Peace Operations: US Costs in Support of Haiti, Former Yugoslavia, Somalia, and Rwanda* (GAO/NSIAD-96-38, March 1996).

The cluster of operations focused on containing and influencing the behavior
of the Saddam Hussein regime in Iraq came nearer to the size that might ap-
proximate a major theater war than did operations in the Balkans. Issued in 1999
with the oxymoronic title of *Major Smaller Scale Contingencies*, an OSD report
listed eight separate operations in Southwest Asia.[14] For most of the 1990s, an
estimated 20,000 United States military personnel served, mainly in Saudi Arabia and Kuwait, in operations associated with the collective $7.44 billion effort.[15]

Table 13. Operational Names for Enforcing International Law and Standards in Southwest Asia

Name	Type	Duration	Authority
Arabian Gulf MIO	Sanctions Enf	1990	UNSCRs 661, 966 (1990)
Determined Response Desert Calm Desert Sortie	multiple (USS *Cole*) (withdraw forces)	2000-	
Desert Farewell	logistics	1992	UN
Desert Fox	Air strikes	1998-99	UN
Desert Shield	defense/security	1990-91	UN
Desert Storm	Offensive	1991	UN

Table 13. Operational Names for Enforcing International Law and Standards in Southwest Asia. (continued)

Name	Type	Duration	Authority
Desert Sabre Desert Sortie Desert Sword			
Patriot Defender	defense/security	1991	
Proven Force			
UNIKOM	peacekeeping	1991	UN
Desert Strike	missile attacks	1996	UN
Desert Thunder	Air strikes	1998	UN
Desert Vigilance	defense/security	1994-95	UN
Desert Viper	show of force	1998	UN
Nordic Knight	defense/security	1998	
Northern Watch	sanctions enf	1992-	UNSCR 688
Constant Vigil Desert Safeguard			
Provide Comfort I and II	humanitarian	1991-96	UNSCR 688
Encourage Hope Express Care			
Pacific Haven		1996-97	
Quick Transit		1996	
Snow Eagle		1992	
Provide Cover	defense/security	1991-	
Southern Watch	sanctions enf	1992-	UNSCRs 687, 688, 949
Desert Falcon		1997-	
Desert Focus		1997-	
Desert Spring		1999	
Guarded Skies			
Gunsmoke		1999	
Intrinsic Action JTF SWA			
Noble Safeguard	defense/security	1999	
Phoenix Jackal Phoenix Scorpion I Phoenix Scorpion II			
Shining Presence	defense/security	1998	
Vigilant Sentinel	show of force	1995	
Vigilant Warrior	show of force	1994	
TLAM Strike (2)	offensive	1993	
TLAM Strike	offensive	1996	

Over the decade, the use of nearly fifty names to designate operations in the Balkans and almost as many names for work in and around Southwest Asia obscured the fact that two major regional campaigns were conducted in the 1990s and remained active when the decade ended. With their ambiguous outcomes, these series of operations resembled but were short of classic combat operations. Both involved long periods of time, high monetary cost, and extensive use of major weapons systems, notably a wide variety of tactical aircraft and Naval combatants. They also resulted in few friendly casualties. American commanders could shuttle active and reserve units into and out of the operations without apparent loss in operational effectiveness. For example, Air National Guard units went into and out of Saudi Arabia on two-week rotations for **Northern Watch** and **Southern Watch,** with some units doing as many as four two-week rotations in three to four years.[16]

While by far the largest efforts of their kind, the decade-long campaigns in the Balkans and in Southwest Asia did not represent the only efforts to uphold international law and standards. The armed forces of the United States played a variety of roles in fourteen other operations of this general type, which are listed in Table 14.

Table 14. The Enforcement of International Law and Standards in Regions other than the Balkans and Southwest Asia				
Name	Region	Type	Duration	Authority
JTF Timor Sea Ops	Southeast Asia	peacekeeping	1999-2000	UN
INTERFET USGET Stabilize				
UNAMIC/UNTAC	Southeast Asia	peacekeeping	1991-93	UN
MFO Sinai	Middle East	peacekeeping	1982-2000	UN
MINURSO	North Africa	peacekeeping	1991-98	UN
UNTSO	Middle East	peacekeeping	1948-	UN
Assured Lift	Sub-Sahara	logistics (peacekeeping)	1997	ECOMOG
Provide Transition	Sub-Sahara	defense/logistics	1992	UN
Restore Hope	Sub-Sahara	peace enforce	1992-93	UN
Continue Hope	Sub-Sahara	multiple types	1993-94	UN
Focus Relief/ UNAMSIL	Sub-Sahara	logistics/training (peacekeeping)	2000	UN
Safe Border (MOMEP)	South America	peacekeeping	1995-99	Latin American nations
Support Democracy	Caribbean	sanctions enforcement	1993-94	UN
Uphold Democracy	Caribbean	peacekeeping	1994-2000	UN
UNOMIG	Georgia	peacekeeping	1993	UN

Overall, the joint operations of the 1990s did not cohere as much by type as by place. Operations came together in a small number of clusters, nearly all relating to each other geographically as they took place in the same region, rather than connecting based on type of mission. The largest groupings were in the Balkans and Southwest Asia. Other substantial sets formed along Caribbean drug shipment routes and in sub-Saharan Africa where numerous noncombatant evacuations and humanitarian missions together with a few stability operations took place.

Even disaster relief operations, the responses to unpredictable meteorological and other natural catastrophes, followed general patterns, with autumn hurricanes in the Caribbean and the southeastern United States, springtime floods along the Mississippi River system, and summer fires in the western forests. Instead of hundreds of disparate operations all over the world, a distribution that would support the views of theorists of global chaos, this handful of operational groups in specific regions yields a more accurate view of a complex decade of operational challenges.

Occurring early in the decade, **Operation Restore Hope** in Somalia,[17] was extremely significant in shaping American views of later military commitments. The operation began as a straightforward humanitarian effort during the last weeks of the Bush administration.[18] The Somali population was reeling from drought; the effects of predatory clan leaders, civil war and anarchy; and the loss of International Monetary Fund aid. In response, non-governmental organizations concentrated their resources on Somalia. The International Red Cross spent nearly half of its worldwide budget trying to get enough food into the country to overwhelm the capacity of clans and gunmen to steal aid shipments as they arrived.[19]

The nature of the American operation changed drastically in the early days of the Clinton presidency when it became clear that a stability operation was necessary since humanitarian aid could not be delivered effectively in the chaotic environment created by the violent conflicts between warring clans. In June 1993, gunmen killed twenty-four United Nations soldiers from Pakistan who were participating in the UN-sponsored attempt to stabilize Somalia. The operation then focused on an American manhunt for Mohamed Farah Aideed, a powerful Somali clan leader in Mogadishu, turning what started as a struggle to deliver food into the most significant operation of the decade in terms of its impact on subsequent American operations. The deaths of eighteen American service members in a single violent encounter with Somali gunmen on October 3, 1993, followed by the macabre display of some of their bodies in the streets of Mogadishu, caused revulsion and a significant backlash in the United States.[20] David Halberstam called it "a devastating setback for humanitarian intervention."[21] In the immediate aftermath of this fight, force protection became the highest priority mission for all United States forces in Somalia. When President Clinton "defined the US mission [in Somalia] as four-fold," on October 7, 1993, his first objective was "protect our troops and our bases ...."[22] If **Desert Storm**, the war against Iraq in 1991, had demonstrated the power of American forces in a conventional conflict, **Restore Hope** in Somalia underscored their vulnerabilities and limitations in an unconventional environment.

The experience in Somalia highlighted the potential consequences of the evolution of an operation into something that was larger and more troublesome than originally anticipated. Any humanitarian operation was susceptible to such change, as the involvement in the solution of one problem either led to the uncovering of another difficulty in need of urgent attention or even caused another problem. After Somalia, this possibility, known to some as "the law of unintended consequences" and characterized by the military as "mission creep," became a major concern.[23]

Ignited by the experience in Somalia, concerns about "force protection," "end states," "exit strategies," and "mission creep" were fueled by memories of the Vietnam conflict, where an advisory effort had expanded into a long war that had consumed over 50,000 American military lives and billions of dollars. These concerns also reflected the relatively low importance of humanitarian and stability operations for the American military. Moreover, the idea of missions that changed and expanded contradicted the view of "normal" civil-military relations in which civilians stated the mission and the military was left to accomplish it, without the substantial further involvement of those who assigned and established the task.[24]

The Department of Defense's *Quadrennial Defense Review* in 1997 downplayed the use of the armed forces for humanitarian emergencies. Ignoring two centuries of American military history, the authors of the study claimed that: "When the interests at stake are primarily humanitarian in nature, the US military is generally not the best means of addressing a crisis." Conceding that it might be "both necessary and appropriate" to use military assets, the report specified that "the military mission should be clearly defined, the risk to American troops should be minimal, and substantial US military involvement should be confined to the initial period of providing relief until broader international assistance efforts get underway." The decision to use military forces would "depend on our ability to identify a clear mission, the desired end state of the situation, and the exit strategy for forces committed."[25]

Occasional military voices, such as that of Marine General Anthony Zinni, who commanded US Central Command from August 1997 to July 2000, noted that missions could evolve with changing situations and that the armed forces were able to adapt rapidly to changing situations. For Zinni, one of the main attributes of the American armed forces was operational flexibility and responsiveness. Distinctions had to be made between mission creep and mission shift as situations could change and new requirements result. General Zinni urged that commanders anticipate the evolution of missions and not dismiss such changes as "mission creep." "Keep the mission focused," he said, "avoiding mission creep, but allow for mission shift (a conscious evolution that responds to the changing situation) …."[26] Nevertheless, the conventional view, as articulated in the *Quadrennial Defense Review*, was of a narrow and restrictive definition of the proper circumstances for the use of military forces in humanitarian and stability operations.[27] At the end of the 1990s, civilian critics decried "force protection fetishism"[28] and "the emerging American way of war—which emphasizes the avoidance of risk and casualties …."[29]

During the decade, American casualties were always attended by substantial press coverage. The most remembered and the most influential such incident was the obscene display of American dead in Mogadishu. Ranged against the relatively low toll in battle deaths in the decade were more than one thousand American military fatalities that occurred during training and non-combat operations. Three operations—**Just Cause**, **Desert Storm**, and **Northern Watch**— had American casualties inflicted accidentally by friendly forces. All of these deaths occurred in the context of a perceived low public tolerance for casualties, inescapable media coverage, and a preoccupation with accounting in detail for all casualties that grew out of the POW/MIA movement following the Vietnam War and was embodied in the agency that searched for the remains of service members missing in action, **Joint Task Force Full Accounting**.[30]

The Somalia experience led to cautious and less direct American participation in humanitarian and stability operations. This effect manifested itself in American commitments worldwide, especially in Africa. After the Rwanda genocide in the spring of 1994, the United States deployed soldiers from US European Command into the border area between Rwanda, Burundi, and the Congo, then still called Zaire, to provide relief support in the massive refugee camps.[31] Known as **Operation Support Hope**, the effort was carefully limited in duration and in extent to preclude any long-term commitment in the region. American forces departed after a few weeks.

In Liberia during 1997 (**Assured Lift**) and in Sierra Leone three years later (**Focus Relief**), the United States played a supporting role, providing logistical help and training for peacekeepers from other nations. These missions mirrored the training missions of the early Cold War when American troops helped train government forces to put down communist insurgencies in Greece and the Philippines; they also recalled earlier experiences with the establishment of native constabularies in the Philippines, Cuba, Haiti, the Dominican Republic, and Nicaragua.[32] Other such operations in the 1990s included contracting and training civilian police for duty in Haiti and Bosnia. American forces in **JTF**

Timor Sea operations in Indonesia supported a peace enforcement effort lead by Australia.[33]

A particularly noteworthy enterprise was **Operation Uphold Democracy** in Haiti.[34] American interest in Haiti and the Caribbean had long and deep roots. Despite the long history of concern, which included major long-term interventions earlier in the twentieth century, **Uphold Democracy** was a singular effort. The operation began on an ambiguous note as American units did not know whether they would enter Haiti as invaders or as invited guests. Only when on the verge of landing in Haiti did their commanders learn that their forces would not be opposed when they arrived.[35] Once on the ground, the American force restored the legitimately elected government and made modest improvements in living conditions in the country.

Two operations resembled the larger efforts in the Balkans and Southwest Asia in their duration, if not in size and complexity. Established in the wake of the 1979 Camp David Accords, the Multinational Force and Observers (MFO) in the Sinai served as a buffer between Israeli and Egyptian forces during Israel's withdrawal from the peninsula. Based on a brigade-sized American contribution, this force remained in place at the end of the twentieth century. In northwestern Africa, the United Nations Mission for the Referendum in Western Sahara (MINURSO), to which the United States made a much smaller commitment, lasted nearly eight years and never involved more than a handful of Americans. Both efforts were reminders of the sometimes inconclusive and extended nature of peace operations.

During the decade, American forces participated in international operations in several modes. Ambassador Richard Holbrooke, who represented the United States at the United Nations in 1999 and 2000, noted three: in the Balkans, the United States operated as an integral part of the international effort; in East Timor, the small United States contingent operated alongside but not under the command of the United Nations force; and in Sierra Leone, the United States did not participate in the actual peacekeeping operation but provided training and financial support.[36] Regardless of the specific form taken by American involvement, at the end of the decade it appeared that as General Zinni observed in a speech at the Naval Institute: "We're going to be doing things like humanitarian operations, consequence management, peace keeping and peace enforcement … operations other than war. These are our future."[37]

Chapter 7
Other Types of Operations

A different category of operation that merits attention was travel by members of the executive branch including cabinet officials, the vice president, the first lady, and particularly the president. Overseas trips by the head of state are integral elements of public diplomacy, highlighting American interest in specific parts of the world. Called "Banner" by Air Mobility Command, these missions are not usually considered in analyses of military operations.[1] However, they not only consume large amounts of military resources, particularly transport aircraft and associated crews and fuel, but also personnel and equipment for security and communications. President Clinton flew to parts of the world rarely visited by American chief executives in the past—Africa twice and Vietnam once. Distant from the United States, these areas had little usable communications infrastructure. Consequently, his entourages were large and imposed significant demands on Air Mobility Command aircraft and crews. During the two Clinton administrations, the upward trend in presidential travel that had started during the first Bush presidency continued and then accelerated.

Table 15. Phoenix Banner (president) and Phoenix Silver (vice president) Airlift Missions, Domestic and Foreign, 1988-1999

Year	Missions	Passengers	Tons of Cargo
CY 1988	477	9,611	5,773
CY 1989	388	10,885	6,859
CY 1990	702	15,169	8,638
CY 1991	555	10,179	6,484
CY 1992	928	11,795	7,901
CY 1993	348	6,065	4,934
CY 1994	598	16,571	12,416
CY 1995	559	14,233	9,535
CY 1996	1,029	25,365	17,826
CY 1997	569	15,056	11,564
CY 1998	929	20,097	17,582
CY 1999	1,240	26,481	20,314

Source: Data provided by United States Transportation Command Research Center, Scott Air Force Base, Illinois, from annual histories of Air Mobility Command and its predecessor, Military Airlift Command.

Public interest in President Clinton's travel peaked in the months after his visit in the spring of 1998 to Rwanda and other East African nations. Particularly expensive and complex because of communications requirements, the visit to six countries cost $42.8 million. The Africa trip involved at least 1,300 government employees, who either accompanied the chief executive or preceded him as members of advance teams. Two months after he returned from this trip, the President went to China, with a smaller retinue of about one thousand people.

The report of a General Accounting Office review of presidential travel in September 1999 noted that the travel was expensive and cost the Department of Defense $292 million for 1997 through 1999. The report also showed that in his first term Clinton and his predecessor, George H. W. Bush, had comparable travel records. President Bush visited 50 countries over 86 days during four years, spending 21.5 days abroad each year; President Clinton went to 49 countries in 81 days during his first term, just under 21 days per year. However, Clinton's second term saw substantial increases, and for his two terms he averaged 28.6 days abroad annually. Overall, Clinton was the most widely traveled president and the first to visit a number of countries and regions, including Botswana, Rwanda, Bulgaria, the Balkans, and northern Vietnam.[2] It was clear that "the scope of detailed planning, magnitude of requirements, and depth of contingency management required to transport the leader of the free world make even the briefest of trips nothing short of a full-blown military operation."[3]

President Clinton's largest trip, to India, Pakistan, and Bangladesh in the early spring of 2000, underscored the impact of presidential travel as a consumer of Department of Defense assets. Known as "**India Banner**," the mission cost a total of $46.5 million, and included 146 cargo flights "to ferry everything from trucks and communications equipment to the presidential limousine." All told, it required 894 sorties and a total of 5,708 flying hours. The simultaneous humanitarian operation called **Atlas Response** in Mozambique, in which the United States joined a number of nations in providing emergency aid after flood waters had submerged much of that country, required 443 sorties and just over one-fourth of the flying hours—1,592—expended on the Clinton visit to India.[4]

Two other types of presidential support operations occurred on a regular and predictable basis. One involved the ceremonies and festivities surrounding the presidential inauguration and primarily occupied elements of the Military District of Washington. In 2001, this mission used just under 1,000 military personnel for about two weeks. The other support activity concerned the shipment of presidential papers and memorabilia to the site of the presidential library. In the case of President Clinton, it took eight flights by Air Mobility Command C-5 aircraft to move more than 660 tons of documents, gifts, artifacts, and other materials from Andrews Air Force Base, Maryland, to Little Rock Air Force Base, Arkansas.[5]

A small number of the operations that took place in the decade did not fit in any of the categories outlined above. **Steel Box** in 1990 and **Auburn Endeavor** in the spring of 1998 involved materials associated with what came to be known as "weapons of mass destruction." **Steel Box** moved chemical munitions from Western Europe and **Auburn Endeavor** removed weapons-grade uranium from former Soviet territory. Other missions ranged from **JTF Olympics**, which supported the 1996 Olympic Summer Games in Atlanta, Georgia, to **Eastern Access**, the reopening and securing of the Navy's Vieques bombing range after Puerto Rican protesters had blocked access. **JTF Panama** removed American forces at the end of the United States presence in the Canal Zone. **Deep Freeze**, the Antarctic research project that had started in 1957, depended on Department of Defense re-supply missions throughout its life and provided a reminder of the role of both the Army and the Navy in nineteenth century scientific research and surveys.

Other operations were singular. **Joint Task Force Full Accounting**, with its headquarters in Hawaii, searched for the remains of American servicemen. **Joint Task Force Computer Network** operations concentrated on protective measures against and responses to cyber-warfare. **Joint Task Force Civil Support** dealt with responses to possible acts of terrorism against the United States. Unlike most joint task forces, which were set up in response to specific short-term emergencies, these organizations were established on a more permanent basis.

Table 16. Miscellaneous Operations

Name	Region	Type	Duration
Auburn Endeavor	Former USSR	Environmental/logistical	1993
Computer Network Def	USA	Electronic security	1999-
Deep Freeze	Antarctica	Scientific/logistical	1957-
Diamante 1	Central America	defense/security	1994-95
Diamante 2	Central America	defense/security	1995-96
Eastern Access	Caribbean	logistics (reopen Viequez)	2000
Full Accounting	Southeast Asia	remains recovery	1992-
Incident Reach	Sub-Sahara	offensive (TLAM)	1998
JTF Bravo	Central America	multiple types	1982-
Encourage Hope			
JTF Civil Support	USA	defense/security	1999-
JTF I (Inauguration)	USA	logistics	2001
JTF Olympics	USA	logistics	1995-96
JTF Panama 99	Central America	logistics (withdrawal)	1999
JTF Philippines	SE Asia	show of force	1989

Table 16. Miscellaneous Operations (continued)			
Name	Region	Type	Duration
Just Cause	Central America	Offensive (with counter-drug component)	1989-90
Northern Denial	North America	defense/security	2000
Passive oversight	Caribbean	defense/security	1997
Presidential Records	North America	logistics	2001
Promote Liberty	Caribbean	peacekeeping	1990-94
Sentinel Lifeguard	Caribbean	show of force	1999
Silent Assurance	SW Asia	defense/security	1997
Steel Box I, II, III	Western Europe	logistics	1990-91
Sustain Liberty	Caribbean	defense/security	1994-97
Taiwan Straits	East Asia	show of force	1996

Operations in this miscellaneous category sometimes involved large numbers of other government agencies along with the Department of Defense. Presidential travel regularly engaged the State Department, the United States Information Agency, the Secret Service, the Immigration and Naturalization Service, and the Customs Service as well as elements of the Department of Defense. **JTF Olympics**, which employed military elements in security and logistical support for the Summer Games in Atlanta in 1996, required coordination with the Federal Bureau of Investigation, the Public Health Service, the Customs Service, and the Federal Aviation Agency. Contacts with nearly sixty Georgia law enforcement agencies were managed through a Law Enforcement Joint Coordination Center. Almost 14,000 military personnel contributed to the effort, including twenty-nine explosive ordnance disposal teams and thirty-two military working dog teams; the cost was $27 million.[6]

Pacific Haven, a mission that was related to **Operation Provide Comfort**, also had the complexity that characterized the more atypical assignments of the period. This operation provided support to Kurdish refugees who had been employed with **Operation Provide Comfort**, the effort to protect and support Kurds who had been driven from their homes in the wake of the war against Iraq, and were, therefore, at risk in their homeland. More than 6,000 refugees were transported to Guam between September 1996 and the end of the operation in the following March; there they were screened before entering the United States. A relatively small operation with a US government price tag of $10 million, **Pacific Haven** involved at least seven other government agencies and a dozen non-governmental organizations. Unlike humanitarian operations, which tended to involve large numbers of non-governmental organizations, and counter-drug efforts, which included a wide variety of law enforcement agencies, these singular missions derived their complexity from the participation of many agencies of the federal government.

Table 17. Non-DOD Participants in Operation Pacific Haven

US Government Agencies

Office of Refugee Resettlement (Department of Health and Human Services)
Office of Foreign Disaster Assistance (Department of State)
Immigration and Naturalization Service
Central Intelligence Agency
Customs Service
Public Health Service

Non-Governmental Organizations

Immigration and Refugee Services of America
Salvation Army
American Red Cross
Refugee Data Center
Lutheran Immigration and Refugee Service
US Catholic Conference
Hebrew Immigrant Aid Society
Church World Service
Ethiopian Community Development Council
InterAction
World Relief
International Rescue Committee

Chapter 8
The Big Picture

Despite the large number of operations, the majority of American personnel in overseas assignments during the decade were on stable tours of duty in places where the American military had long been assigned. Given the proliferation of operational names and frequent press speculation that use of United States military forces in many small operations might degrade their ability to respond to a serious crisis, it is important to note that most overseas stationing of troops followed the Cold War pattern. The bulk of the armed forces serving overseas were in routine assignments in the same places—Germany, Korea, Japan, Okinawa—where they had been stationed during much of the Cold War.[1] Moreover, in the 1980s, when the armed forces ranged in size from just under 2.1 million to almost 2.2 million, a larger portion (ranging from 23.8 percent to 25.3 percent) as well as a larger absolute number was regularly deployed outside the United States than during the post-Cold War decade.

Table 18. Overseas Deployment, Ashore and Afloat, 1980-2000		
Year	Active Force	Deployed
1980	2,050,826	488,726 (23.8%)
1981	2,082,897	501,832 (24.1%)
1982	2,108,612	528,484 (25.1%)
1983	2,123,349	519,517 (24.5%)
1984	2,138,157	510,730 (23.9%)
1985	2,151,032	515,367 (24.0%)
1986	2,169,112	526,328 (24.3%)
1987	2,174,217	523,702 (24.1%)
1988	2,138,213	540,588 (25.3%)
1989	2,130,229	509,873 (23.9%)
1990	2,046,144	609,422 (29.8%)
1991	1,986,259	447,572 (22.5%)
1992	1,807,177	344,065 (19.0%)
1993	1,705,103	308,020 (18.1%)
1994	1,610,490	286,594 (17.8%)
1995	1,518,224	238,064 (15.7%)

Table 18. Overseas Deployment, Ashore and Afloat, 1980-2000 (continued)		
Year	Active Force	Deployed
1996	1,471,722	240,421 (16.3%)
1997	1,438,562	227,258 (15.8%)
1998	1,406,830	259,871 (18.5%)
1999	1,385,703	252,763 (18.2%)
2000	1,384,338	257,817 (18.6%)

Source: "Active Force" and "Deployed" data provided by the Directorate for Information Operations and Reports, Washington Headquarters Services, Office of the Secretary of Defense, and is for 30 September of each year, except for the year 2000, which is reported as of 30 June.

Beginning in 1994, the Joint Staff tracked the number of service members deployed on operations. Those "deployed" on current operations, as opposed to those "stationed" overseas, never represented as much as 5 percent of the active-duty force. Increasing numbers of deployed service members came from the reserve components; this was especially true for the Air Force and the Army. At the end of the 1990s, the Army began to rely heavily on the Army Reserve and the Army National Guard to provide forces for duty in the Balkans.[2] At the end of every fiscal year except 1994, when substantial numbers of military personnel were serving in Haiti, the overwhelming majority of those involved in current operations were concerned with one of the two major clusters of operations, either in Southwest Asia or the Balkans. A historical example of a force truly stressed by overseas deployments is provided by a British army at the end of the nineteenth century that had 104,000 men, nearly half of its 212,000 soldiers, deployed abroad.[3] It was, in the words of General Sir Garnet Wolseley, "a squeezed lemon."[4]

Despite the small portion of the force deployed on current operations outside of the United States, these missions raised the question of whether the employment of American forces in stability operations and other gendarme operations represented a legitimate use of the military. The discussion focused on whether such use would degrade training and wear down equipment and people, eroding combat effectiveness. Included in the debate was the question of wheth-er frequent deployments would cause service members to leave the service.

Viewed from the perspective of aggregate numbers alone, the issues gener-ated by deployments in this decade could be considered marginal, but much of the discussion proceeded without informed reference to numbers. Many ana-lysts knew little more than the total size of the force and the number of troops cut in the years following the end of the Cold War. When it came to the overall magnitude of deployments, precision frequently went out of the window.

Table 19. Portion of Active Force Outside of the United States and Assigned to Operations from 1994 to 2000

Year	Total Strength	On Duty in Foreign Countries and Areas	Deployed on Current Operations	In SW Asia	In the Balkans	SW Asia and Balkans as % of all Deployed
1994	1,610,490	286,594 (17.8%)	67,731 (4.2%)	20,878	5,826	39.4%
1995	1,518,224	238,064 (15.7%)	36,786 (2.4%)	25,225	4,956	82.0%
1996	1,471,722	240,421 (16.3%)	62,990 (4.3%)	31,152	24,911	89.0%
1997	1,438,562	227,258 (15.8%)	35,145 (2.4%)	12,756	18,062	87.7%
1998	1,406,780	259,871 (18.5%)	43,067 (3.1%)	25,799	13,472	91.2%
1999	1,385,703	252,763 (18.2%)	47,975 (3.5%)	27,236	16,701	91.6%
2000	1,372,900	238,047 (17.3%)	39,049 (2.8%)	20,875	15,908	94.2%

Source: "Total Strength" and "On Duty in Foreign Countries and Areas" data provided by the Directorate for Information Operations and Reports, Washington Headquarters Services, Office of the Secretary of Defense, and is for 30 September of each year, except for the year 2000, which is reported as of 30 June. Data concerning personnel "Deployed on Current Operations" is provided by J-1 of the Joint Staff on a weekly basis and is taken from the report for the last week of September except for the year 2000, for which the last week of June is used. "Personnel Deployed on Current Operations" is a subset of personnel "On Duty in Foreign Countries and Areas." All percentages are based on the "Total Strength" of the **active force** for each respective year.

James Kitfield, a civilian writer who wrote often on military issues and strongly supported military claims that new missions were causing great strain, asserted that "the pace of deployments increase[d] by more than 300 percent since 1989."[5] Major General Arnold Fields, the Director of the Marine Corps Staff, claimed in 2000 that the pace of deployments had increased "16-fold" since the end of the Cold War.[6] A *New York Times* reporter added that "the number of peacekeeping missions, relief efforts and other military operations has proliferated."[7] Basing their assessments on unclassified slides posted on "defenselink," the Department of Defense website, operations research analysts accepted without comment the assertion that "over the past 10 years the military has downsized at a time when operations tempo and OOTW [Operations Other Than War] have dramatically increased."[8] Paul Mann declared that "US Armed Forces have been ordered overseas with much higher frequency in the past 10 years than during the near half-century after World War II." Mann asserted that, "In the decade since 1990, deployments numbered more than 60. They totaled fewer than 50 in the entire 45 years from 1945-90, according to congressional figures."[9] Drawn from a Congressional Research Service report, *Instances of Use of United States Armed Forces Abroad, 1798-1989*, written by Ellen Collier, the "congressional figures" counted the entire Korean War as one deployment and the 1964-1973 conflict in Vietnam as another. Post-Cold War practice gave more than forty names to the cluster of operations in the Balkans that was, in the aggregate, far smaller than either the Korean War or the Vietnam conflict.[10] Clearly, all deployments were not equal, although the 1990's practice of naming them could give the impression that they were.[11] Merely counting post-Cold War operations did not acknowledge the fact that they varied widely in size, duration, importance, and allocation of forces.[12]

The post-Cold War approach to naming operations was part of the problem. The war in Vietnam, which was the focus of operations from the early 1960s to the 1970s, encompassed about twenty operations with English-language names every year in the late 1960s. Like deployments in the post-Cold War decade, these named operations varied widely. There were ground offensives, air strikes, pacification missions, and even humanitarian operations that provided medical care and emergency relief to civilians. However, the number and diversity of individual operations never obscured the identity of the overall conflict; they were all part of the Vietnam War.[13]

Missing from the commentary on and analyses of post-Cold War operations were two basic facts: seldom, if ever, did the actual number of service members deployed on operations exceed 5 percent of the total force; and much of the operational activity occurred in two large, complex, and expensive operational clusters in the Balkans and in Southwest Asia. Despite the many names, the focus and locations of the operations were restricted.

The military services used complex methods to measure the extent of their overseas commitments. Instead of using overall service strength as the baseline against which to compute the level and impact of deployments, all four services based their calculations on what they considered to be their deployable force—a much smaller figure than their total strengths. Moreover, all four services used different processes to compute their baselines—methods which incorporated some abstruse methods of counting. The Marines and the Army added to the number of deployed personnel those individuals in training overseas but subtracted from the deployable force those in training in the United States, reducing the baseline by the number of trainees at home and inflating the size of the deployed group by the number of trainees abroad. Since they began tracking the numbers at different times, it was impossible to make comparisons over the entire decade.[14]

Some statements that could be used to support claims of over-extension were truly misleading. In May 1997, the Army announced that its soldiers served for the first time in one hundred foreign countries, a total that had increased from eighty the preceding year. The total number involved in this global activity at the end of the fiscal year amounted to 31,000 soldiers. Moreover, 74 of the countries listed by the Army had nine or fewer soldiers for a total of 270; an average of about 3.65 service members per country, many of whom were probably attachés and members of attaché staffs, routinely assigned to United States embassies.[15] The bulk of deployed Army personnel were in Germany (44,000) and Korea (29,000), just as they had been during the Cold War.[16]

More recently, the newsletter of the Association of the United States Army, *Defense Report*, noted that "thousands of soldiers do the day-to-day work of engagement," and cited the Army role in Hungary, Turkey, Moldova, East Timor, Micronesia, Australia, Japan, and Haiti.[17] Indeed, there were Army representatives in all of these nations at the end of calendar year 2000. However, the 1,740 soldiers in Japan reflected the long-standing, post-World War II commitment of forces to that country, and the 28 in Micronesia had nothing to do with engagement, since Micronesia, which is also known as the Trust Territory of the Pacific Islands, belongs to the United States. The other deployments ranged from moderately small levels relating to current operations—360 in Hungary, mainly in support of Balkan operations, and 190 in Turkey, largely associated with operations against Saddam Hussein's regime—to 11 in Australia; nine in Indonesia, including East Timor; nine in Haiti; and three in Moldova.[18]

The Navy, like the Air Force, seeking to hold deployments of individual sailors to a maximum of six months while adhering to a regular schedule of ship maintenance, deployed two aircraft carriers in the Persian Gulf and claimed as a result that some ship upkeep and crew training had to be curtailed. One expert argued that the operational availability of carriers varied from one in three to one in four, depending on the location, making each operational deployment represent something like a $20 billion investment, each deployed carrier representing an expense of between $6 billion and $7 billion.[19]

During the 1990s, in response to changing operational imperatives, the Navy increasingly relied on amphibious ships rather than on aircraft carriers. Carrier participation in operations declined from 78 percent in 1977-1984 to about 50 percent in 1990-1996.[20] Only one humanitarian response operation involved aircraft carriers. Multiple eruptions of Mount Pinatubo on Luzon in June 1991 were followed by cascades of ash that covered the Clark Field airbase so densely that it collapsed several roofs. The smoke, ash, and other debris also forced closure of all island airports, so the operation, known as **Fiery Vigil**, included at least one carrier battle group, totaling more than 10,000 sailors, in the rescue of nearly 20,000 American nationals. The aircraft carriers USS *Abraham Lincoln* and USS *Midway* removed thousands of people, with 3,600 sailing on the *Lincoln* to the island of Cebu where they were flown to Guam.[21] Carriers were still used extensively; during 1993-1994, the Navy rotated at least seven carriers into **Operation Southern Watch**.

Despite the apparently small portion of the total force deployed at any time, personnel tempo (perstempo) and operational tempo (optempo) were important. Concerns were, in part, a response to the change in the nature of deployments. In some operations, the situation more closely resembled the experience of the Indian-fighting Army than that of the Cold War force, with little detachments at widely scattered and remote stations responding to small emergencies as they popped up, rather than larger forces located mainly at permanent stations with substantial facilities. The experience of the 22nd Marine Expeditionary Unit in 1996-1998 with six noncombatant evacuations, executed or planned, surely fit this pattern.

Frequent deployments created disruption and austerity for those involved. Air Force pilots coped with the boring routine of policing the no-fly zones over Iraq and the stark living conditions of the expeditionary environment in Saudi Arabia. Accustomed to operating as a Cold War garrison force with service members accompanied by families and working out of large and comfortable permanent bases, the Air Force faced the frequent need to send parts of aviation units to austere Persian Gulf installations which "disrupted home base operations and disrupted personal lives." As Lieutenant General Patrick Gamble observed in 1998, "My impression ... is that the real cost we're paying is a turbulence factor in rear areas, combined with no light at the end of the tunnel."[22]

Optempo and perstempo issues clearly had an impact on some elements of the armed forces as a variety of units and types of equipment were regularly in high demand. According to the General Accounting Office, they were "major platforms, weapons systems, units, and/or personnel that possess unique mission capabilities and are in continual high demand to support worldwide joint military operations."[23] Priorities for the use of such assets ranked war at the top of the list; then other military operations that might involve hostile contact, such as peacekeeping; then training; and finally counter drug operations.[24]

In a major change from the Cold War years, assets that were in high demand were usually not major combat formations. This was especially true in the Army, where demand was extremely high for military police, aviation, civil affairs units, and special operations forces.[25] But it was also true for the other services for whom specialized aircraft, including EA-6B aircraft which were used to suppress enemy air defenses and electronically jam anti-aircraft radar, as well as Airborne Warning and Control Systems (AWACS) aircraft, U-2 reconnaissance planes, and F-16 CJ fighter aircraft equipped with anti-radar missiles were in short supply.[26]

Among ground forces, military police units were in very high demand throughout the 1990s, for operations in the United States as well as abroad. **Joint Task Force Andrew**, the military response to Hurricane Andrew in 1992, included eight Army Military Police companies among the 106 units from all services that deployed.[27] In Bosnia, three years later, MP units replaced some infantry and armor formations after six months, as it became clear that they were more appropriate for the mission. In Rwanda in 1994, where the 325th

Airborne Infantry Regiment provided security for military units that produced safe drinking water and participated in the relief effort, it became apparent that Military Police could have performed these roles.[28] Two years later, in the wake of the June 1996 terrorist bombing of the Khobar Towers, at least 64 one- and two-person bomb-sniffing dog teams, from the Army, Navy, and the Air Force, went to Saudi Arabia as part of **Operation Desert Focus**.

In the middle of the decade, the demand for military police severely strained the Army's ability to provide them. During the period from October 1994 through December 1995, US Army Forces Command military police assets were fully committed to operational requirements. Two brigades, six battalions, twenty-six companies, and one Prisoner of War Internment Center were either deployed outside the continental United States or had just returned from overseas duty. The MP companies were deployed, on the average, for 147 days during fiscal year 1995, with an average interval between deployments of only 8.4 months.[29]

Even missions not associated with the operations in the Balkans or Southwest Asia made major demands on military police assets. **Sea Signal/JTF 160**, which involved operating and securing camps for as many as 50,000 Cuban and Haitian refugees, at Guantanamo, Cuba, and in Panama, employed 14 military police companies, three battalion headquarters, and a brigade headquarters, a total of 18 of the 55 Army units deployed. Since 1982, **Joint Task Force Bravo** had provided an American presence in Honduras that expanded and contracted in response to natural disasters and provided training to reserve component units; the operation employed four MP companies on three-month tours of duty. **Sustain Liberty** in Panama required four MP companies on six-month assignments.[30]

The emergence of military police in a position of prominence in post-Cold War operations seemed to affect the morale of unit members positively. Writing in the *Washington Post*, Thomas Ricks observed that, "Of the roughly 5,600 US troops on the peacekeeping mission in Kosovo, the happiest appear to be the 500 military police." Ricks noted that the military police enjoyed being "at the center of the international effort, patrolling constantly and interacting with the population." On the other hand, he wrote, "The infantry and other combat units, by contrast, tend to hate it." The central role of MPs, who were "old hands at using the least amount [of force] necessary to get the job done, a key skill here," changed traditional roles in which infantry, armor, and aviation tended to get the most attention and play the central parts. "MPs," Ricks wrote of operations in Kosovo, "head out to patrol the exotic towns and snow-capped mountains of this Balkan province, while tank crews pull boring guard duty at the dusty main gate" of Camp Bondsteel.[31]

Toward the end of the decade, the central role of military police received increased attention. The British army had discovered some decades ago that, "speaking generally, the tank is an unnecessarily powerful weapon for police work and has the disadvantage of noisiness; and in many areas the use of heavy armored vehicles is restricted by the nature of bridges which exist or could be constructed with limited resources."[32] As one American observer recently noted, police were in fact best suited for police work: "the Army already has units whose doctrine, equipment and training fit them almost perfectly for constabulary operations. They're called military police ...."[33] The Army began to consider expanding the size, structure, and role of MPs in military operations abroad. There were two police issues: force protection and crime. Military police increasingly seemed to provide the right answer to the former and perhaps to the latter as well. With future threats coming from thugs, ethnic cleansing within terrified populations suspicious of authority, and terrorists, military police seemed right for the job, and Major General Thomas J. Plewes, Chief of the Army Reserve, argued that military police were needed more than ever.[34]

Training increasingly took into account the use of military police in gendarme operations. A four-day session for 2,575 reservists of the 800th MP Brigade at Fort A. P. Hill, an exercise known as **Gold Sword IV**, was "intended to test military units charged with running camps that handle prisoners of war, civilian internees and refugees .... The growing occurrence of humanitarian efforts, like the Bosnia and Haiti missions, has demanded that training focus on managing civilian refugees, said Lieutenant Colonel David L. Parker, commander of one of the [four] camps."[35]

Meanwhile, the United Nations department of peacekeeping operations scrambled to assemble the thousands of police officers needed for its operations in the Balkans, East Timor, several war zones in Africa, Cyprus, Tajikistan, Haiti, and Guatemala. Few civilian police departments had officers to spare to meet the high demand for civilian as well as military police. Nevertheless, from 1989 forward, most United Nations operations used some civilian police, who were limited to monitoring and supervising indigenous law enforcement agencies. In Somalia, where attempts to create a semblance of order foundered, some observers considered creation of a national police force or gendarmerie to be one of the first essential steps in establishing the rudiments of civil society.[36] Ruth Wedgwood, a Council on Foreign Relations expert on the United Nations, complained "Every time there's been any question of where to put together a really robust police force, everybody has ducked." She thought the issue was "something that the Pentagon and NATO really have to face up to," because "the United Nations does not have the military."[37] Realistically, law enforcement resources of all types were overburdened and adequate police resources were not available to either the United Nations or the United States.

The United States Marine Corps took steps to add military police training and personnel to their deployable units. Like the Army, the Marines began to appreciate that police work could lie at the center of future missions. Consequently, the Corps began modest restructuring of its brigade-sized Marine Expeditionary Units (MEUs) to include expanded police capabilities. In the early months of 2000, the units that deployed from Camp LeJeune, North Carolina—the 22nd, 24th, and 26th MEUs—had six or seven members with police training, typically led by a sergeant or staff sergeant. The Camp Pendleton, California, expeditionary units—the 11th, 13th, and 15th—had restructured to increase the deploying military police presence to as many as 14 Marines led by a staff non-commissioned officer. When the 11th MEU deployed, it had a captain serving as force protection/anti-terrorism officer and a military police trained lieutenant, with a sergeant and a detachment of 12 school-trained military police.[38]

By the end of the decade, restructuring the Marine military police community and enhancing the military police presence within Marine expeditionary units was close to realization. The Corps' three-star generals had approved creation of military police battalions within three units, with battalions in turn creating detachments for various tactical units, such as the 2nd Marine Division at Camp Lejeune or 11th MEU at Camp Pendleton. The goal was to restructure by 2002. All three of the new battalions had identical structures but with fewer people than stateside military police battalions. This structure allowed deployment of half platoons of 20 Marines led by a police-trained lieutenant, adding seven military police to the largest MEU detachments and as many as 14 to the others.[39] American ground forces were starting to adapt to the reality of post-Cold War operations.[40]

Adaptation did not come without disagreement over where the emphasis should be. In July 2000, the General Accounting Office examined the issue of high demand-low density assets for the Subcommittee on Military Readiness and Management Support of the Senate Committee on Armed Services. The inquiry focused on "six military assets that have been heavily used in contingency operations in a series of case studies," but when it came to land forces, the GAO emphasized Army divisions and civil affairs forces rather than military police. Operations in the Balkans employed forces from four of the Army's ten active divisions and one of the eight National Guard divisions by the end of 1999. Regarding civil affairs units, the report noted that the Army did not have enough capability to meet its requirements but was optimistic about an improved supply of these specialists in the future.[41]

Otherwise, the General Accounting Office focused its report on specialized aircraft that belonged to the Navy, Marine Corps and Air Force. Prominent among these was the EA-6B (Prowler), whose mission was suppression of enemy air defenses by electronically jamming anti-aircraft radar and communications. Both aircraft and crews were in short supply, so much so that the combined demand for these aircraft for **Operations Northern Watch** and **Southern Watch** and for **Noble Anvil** forced closure of classes at the Whitbey Island Electronic Attack Weapons School so instructors could deploy. At one point, 17 of the Marine Corps's 20 EA-6Bs were operationally engaged.[42] For three other seriously over committed aircraft types—AWACS, U-2s, and F16 CJs—the problem was similar. There were simply not enough crews, and those that were available deployed beyond the standard of 120 days per year set by both the Navy and the Air Force.[43] The Joint Staff agreed with the GAO on the shortages of these and other specialized planes, helicopters, and unmanned aerial vehicles.[44]

Because so many operations responded to humanitarian emergencies or at least had a humanitarian component, medical resources were frequently in high demand. Fifteen of the 106 units that deployed to Florida as part of **JTF Andrew** were medical, among them air ambulance, entomology, and public health personnel. The Air Force's Critical Care Air Transport Team from Lackland Air Force Base, Texas, went to eastern Africa in August 1998, after the bombings of the American embassies in Nairobi, Kenya, and Dar es Salaam, Tanzania, as part of **Operation Resolute Response**. Prior to that assignment, the unit had deployed 35 times in 1996, to Central and South America as well as Europe.[45]

Medical units generally responded to two sets of needs, those of the population in the area affected by a disaster and those of the American troops sent into unfamiliar environments that usually also had significant deficiencies in sanitation and public health. In Haiti, 13 of the 35 Army units from Forces Command that went into the operation were medical units. They went in two groups of six, with one company of an area support medical battalion overlapping the assignment of each group. The six in each set—the first went in January through June 1995 and the second in June-November 1995—included one hospital, one medical logistics company, one veterinary detachment, one combat stress detachment, one sanitation/entomology detachment, and an air ambulance company.[46]

Where the disaster responses involved a significant construction component, engineer units were heavily involved. During **JTF Andrew**, nineteen deploying units—almost one out of every nine—were either Navy Seabees or Army engineers. They included combat and construction units, a bridge-building company, firefighters, and divers.[47] The frequent demand for forces usually seen as support elements—military police, engineers (including Navy Seabees), civil affairs, medical, and public affairs units—seemed to turn the conventional idea of "tooth and tail," which held that combat arms forces were the main deployed forces and that others supported and sustained them, on its head. Even though **Desert Storm** very early in the decade was the only operation that approximated a major regional war, the Department of Defense adhered to the traditional notion of "tooth and tail" in its efforts to "preserve the critical capabilities of our military forces—'the tooth'—while reducing infrastructure and support activities—'the tail'—wherever prudent and possible."[48]

Strategic airlift represented a critical part of any deployment. Analysts frequently noted the central importance of air transportation in moving forces and equipment into operations.[49] General Anthony Zinni, whose Central Command often drew heavily on such support, told an interviewer that "Strategic airlift in general is our number one concern and the area we place as our top requirement, and airlift as a whole."[50] Partly because of the dependence on movement of people and supplies by air and partly because of the preference for air operations over the commitment of ground combat forces, the Air Force appeared to be more heavily taxed by operational requirements than the other services.[51]

Although some shortages, such as those in airlift and medical support, occurred regularly, certain operations imposed large demands on assets that were seldom strained. For example, **Operation Joint Endeavor**, the first in the long series of peacekeeping operations in Bosnia—it was followed in order by **Joint Guard**, **Joint Forge**, and **Joint Guardian** and their variously named ground, air, and sea components—put a severe strain on public affairs units. Fourteen separate public affairs organizations, 12 from the Army and two from the Air Force, totaling more than 200 people, went to the Balkans.[52] **Restore Hope** in Somalia had a public affairs staff of sixty. These large commitments of public affairs elements and specialists reflected what Charles Moskos called a reversal in the historic pattern of media build-up, which traditionally came after a military action started. In modern gendarme operations (Moskos called them "operations other than war"), commercial media organizations mobilized at least as rapidly as the military force, carried extraordinarily sophisticated equipment to record and immediately transmit images, and sometimes beat the military to the area of operations. Not all operations called for deployment of large contingents of public affairs personnel. The involvement of 24,000 Army troops in the response to Hurricane Andrew in the United States in August-October 1992 led to the deployment of only one public affairs unit, a press camp headquarters detachment.[53]

The addition of so many public affairs units to the force that went to Bosnia may have been due to the politically sensitive nature of the deployment, but the lessons of Somalia in 1992 and Haiti in 1994 may also have played a role. In the Somalia operation, photographers and reporters, intentionally alerted by official press briefings in Washington to an impending nighttime amphibious operation, had waited for armed reconnaissance parties to hit the beach, then blinded them with television lights. In Haiti, media representatives agreed to refrain from illuminating any airborne assault, but still appeared in such large numbers that they interfered with the soldiers' work. The commander of

Atlantic Command complained to the Chairman of the Joint Chiefs of Staff of the "lack of restraint on the part of reporters covering the operation," noting that "we've seen photographers wander dangerously close to automatic weapons fire–watched camera crews weaving their way through troops working to secure an area." With anywhere from 1,000 to 1,300 media representatives watching the operation and searching for stories, commanders "even witnessed reporters interviewing soldiers as actions are ongoing."[54] Public affairs organizations were needed to create space in which units could operate.

All of the services initiated some responses to changing operational requirements. Midway through the decade, just after the large deployment to Haiti, the smaller mission to Rwanda, and in the middle of a period of intense counter-drug and immigrant interdiction activity, the Army was beginning to try to adjust to the new environment. General William Hartzog, the commander of Training and Doctrine Command and formerly the deputy commander of US Atlantic Command during the Haiti operation, convened "a general-officer level conference" in April 1995, to discuss recent operational experiences, "in an effort to understand more clearly the unique operational challenges that OOTW [operations other than war] present and to ensure that the United States Army is developing force structure and personnel with the capabilities and skills needed to meet these challenges …."[55] The Army's effort continued through the decade, with emphasis on considering lighter, more flexible forces than the large infantry and armor divisions that had been the mainstays of the Cold War force. Toward the end of the decade, the Defense Science Board saw a new interest in "transformation-related initiatives" and expressed optimism concerning the focus of all of the services on "advanced concept development and experimentation …."[56]

While all of the services considered changes, the Air Force implemented the most far-reaching structural modification. In addition to reducing aircrew deployments to Southwest Asia from ninety to forty-five days and reassigning air crews to high demand/low density aircraft, such as AWACS, HC-130s, and U-2s, in 2000 the Air Force rearranged its deployable force into ten Air Expeditionary Forces to manage the high demand for air transport and various combat aircraft. The ten Air Expeditionary Forces rotated primary responsibility for missions every ninety days. Each contained 175 aircraft, for combat, transport, refueling, and surveillance. Each was on alert for ninety days, so that the burden of responding to contingencies was shared and so the disruption caused by deployments could be controlled and made more predictable.[57]

Other structural and organizational adaptations took place within the service organizational structures with little notice or fanfare. The presence of Marines trained as military police in the Marine Expeditionary Unit is a case in point. The change in the way Army lawyers viewed their role also illustrates the evolution of views in response to mission changes. As early as 1983, in the aftermath of **Operation Urgent Fury** in Grenada, the Judge Advocate General Corps saw the need to move beyond traditional roles in courts martial, claims, and legal assistance to service members, into complex areas such as rules of engagement, pre-deployment legal assistance with wills and powers of attorney, advising commanders on combat targeting and contracting, assisting in investigation of war crimes and friendly fire incidents, and drafting war trophy policies. By the middle of the 1990s, with the experience of the war against Iraq and operations in Somalia and Haiti, these changes within the Judge Advocate General Corps were essentially complete.[58] The Army lawyers' adaptation took place quietly and professionally. During the decade, in response to new requirements, the missions of certain specialists changed and expanded without any apparent problems.

Major changes also took place in the use of reserve forces. Under the "Total Force" policy that emerged after the Vietnam War, US forces, particularly the Army and the Air Force, were structured so that they needed substantial reinforcement by reserve forces to conduct a major operation effectively. Still, reserve forces were exactly that, additional organizations and personnel designed to augment combat forces and provide combat support and combat service support elements required to sustain the active force in the event of emergencies. The force that went to war against Iraq in 1990-1991 made significant use of Reserve and National Guard augmentation within this post-Vietnam framework.[59]

Some use of reserve forces in the 1990s fit the post-Vietnam pattern. The Air Force, for example, repeatedly sent Air Guard fighter units to Southwest Asia to augment the active squadrons enforcing the no-fly zones over Iraq. In addition, Air Force reserve component transport units frequently became involved in delivery of emergency supplies during humanitarian operations. In other cases that remained within the traditional framework of reserve usage, specialists such as Army civil affairs officers were frequently called to duty.[60]

However, the deployment of Army National Guard combat brigades to operations in the Balkans represented a major departure from previous practice under the "Total Force" framework.[61] More than 700 soldiers of the 49th Armored Division went to Bosnia for six months in the summer of 2000, as both the headquarters and major troop component for American peacekeepers in Bosnia. The Army National Guard did not go to Bosnia to augment active forces; it went in lieu of them. It was the first such use for a major combat formation of the Army Guard, and it was accompanied by a general rise in the use of Army Reserve and National Guard forces. Subsequent unit rotations also included National Guard headquarters elements and general officers, marking a significant change from the use of reserve component forces during the war against Iraq, when the Army resorted to provisional commands under senior active component officers rather than activate reserve component organizations commanded by reserve component generals.[62]

Contracting offered another way to reduce the operational burden. The use of civilian firms to perform support and logistical tasks, ranging from camp construction to port operations and from food service to motor pool management, had ample historical precedent and became big business during the Vietnam War. During the 1990s, contractor operations ranged from general logistical support to provision of specific types of technical support, such as Serbo-Croatian translators. Brown and Root, which had been one of the principals in the RMK-BRJ construction consortium that built American military facilities in Vietnam, had a substantial role in numerous post-Cold War operations, starting with provision of support to troops in Somalia during **Operation Support Hope**.[63] This firm's involvement peaked in a group of huge contracts dating from 1995 and totaling over $2 billion, to develop infrastructure and support American troops in Bosnia and Kosovo during **Operations Joint Endeavor**, **Joint Forge**, and **Joint Guardian**.[64]

Adjustments in response to the post-Cold War operational environment also were implemented or at least considered at the joint level. The global military force policy, established by the Joint Staff in July 1996, was intended to allocate scarce assets among theater commanders for use in crises, contingencies, and long-term joint task force operations, based on mission priorities, validated requirements, and availability. The military services identified assets to be included under the policy and determined the rate at which these assets could be deployed without adversely affecting unit readiness and quality of life. The goal was to meet the theater commanders' requirements, while assuring that assets were maintained at the highest possible level of readiness and availability to respond to crises.[65]

Early assessments of the impact of the policy were optimistic. The 1997 *Quadrennial Defense Review* reported that the policy "had dramatically improved management of AWACS deployments, stabilized RC-135 and EP-3 deployments at a steady-state rate, and improved the deployments rate for EA-6Bs" and that initial success was leading to development of a more comprehensive system "to monitor the effects of high operating tempo."[66] A report on contingency operations two years later echoed this confident tone.[67] Nevertheless, after air operations over Yugoslavia in 1999, the over commitment of scarce aircraft assets again became an issue.[68]

Admiral James O. Ellis, commander of US Naval forces in Europe, proposed another approach to the issue of operational tempo. Ellis, who also commanded **JTF Noble Anvil** during **Operation Allied Force**, the bombing operations of the spring of 1999 in Yugoslavia, urged development of a plan for a fully functional joint task force and component staffs, a kind of "JTF in a Box." The concept included construction of facilities, creation of a training program, and development of procedures, as well as a database for tracking the availability of potential staff members.[69] Such a concept had been tried earlier in the Army Corps of Engineers, where it had foundered because the lists of potential staff members for so-called "redi districts," that were intended to handle emergency construction, had not been kept up to date.[70]

Programs such as the global force policy and proposals for deployable organizations responded directly to conditions that were prevalent during the first half of the decade. Two analysts, Billy Brooks and Kevin Roller, noted "more peace keeping, peace-enforcement, and humanitarian assistance operations were initiated during 1991-95 than during any of the three previous five-year time periods since 1975."[71] Moreover, the operations raised questions concerning specific American interests and the effectiveness of military forces in such operations. Haiti, Rwanda, and especially Somalia did not respond quickly to the application of the military forces the United States employed. These missions, as Brooks and Roller noted, "were not amenable to decisive and quick action." They tended to stretch out in time, like the peacekeeping mission in the Sinai Peninsula (**Multinational Force and Observers** or **MFO**) that dated from 1982 and the subsequent operations in the Balkans.[72]

Overall, the decade seemed to be marked by a major contradiction between the demands of gendarme operations and domestic political concerns. Gendarme operations, whether they concerned law enforcement, peacekeeping in all of its varieties, nationbuilding, or disaster relief and humanitarian work, were messy, frequently did not promise clear end states, and could be marked by changes in missions and increased expenditures. Law enforcement, particularly the pursuit of diverse villains such as Manuel Noriega, Mohamed Farah Aideed, and Slobodan Milosovic, could take startling and violent turns. Such operations, whether involving drug interdiction, illegal immigrants, or the crimes of dictators and terrorists, rarely allow clearly defined exit strategies, schedules, and end states, all of which were elements of domestic political demands for clarity and finality. Nor could such operations meet the desire to avoid casualties, what Max Boot called "bodybag syndrome."[73]

In the emphasis on operations that did not resemble conventional wars, the decade resembled several periods of American history when the gendarme function had predominated. The twelve years between **Operation Just Cause** and 9/11 were marked by complex operations with military personnel working with international organizations, allies, contractors, and private charitable organizations, always under intense media scrutiny. Sometimes bombing and distribution of humanitarian assistance went on simultaneously, much to the discomfiture of relief agencies, who complained about blurring distinctions between fighters and aid workers and who required confidence in their neutrality on the part of belligerents. Thus in Kosovo NATO built refugee camps in Macedonia and Albania while American planes dropped bombs as part of the same operation.[74]

Overall, complexity and diversity were the hallmarks of this decade. Even taking into account the tendency to exaggerate the amount of work, the operational tempo remained high, while the demand for forces moved away from traditional large combat formations. Above all, the multiple missions of the period touched virtually all regions of the globe.

Chapter 9
Transition to the Future

In some respects the discussions and debates and projections all became irrelevant on Tuesday, 11 September 2001, when the United States was attacked by terrorists who commandeered four American airliners and crashed them with devastating results. All of the compelling issues of the preceding twelve years—casualty avoidance, the preference for remotely fired, precision-guided weapons rather than ground forces, operational tempo, exit strategies and end states—were moot, at least for the moment. Discussion of substantial reductions in the budget and personnel of the Defense Department ended. All involved in national defense turned their attention to identifying, dealing with, and punishing the perpetrators of the attacks of September 11. Reserves were called to duty, money was appropriated, and the old questions lost their importance. The immediate post-Cold War era of operations ended when the 9/11 catastrophe took place.

Yet the period that started at the end of 1989 and ended in September of 2001 still merits attention as it provides numerous examples of the conduct of many kinds of missions. Study of these operations raises the question of how an era that shared so many elements with much of America's military history could have been considered so unique. Review of the period also raises the question of why there was widespread acceptance of the idea that during the period American military forces were overextended, when the numbers do not support such a claim.

The period of 1989-2001 put a premium on types of military forces that had previously not been in the highest demand or of the highest concern. Military police, engineers, medical and civil affairs units all were in high demand as were airlift assets as well as specialized reconnaissance and combat aircraft. Heavy combat forces were used for missions more appropriate for other formations partly because they were more numerous and, therefore, more available than units more suited to the tasks. After September 2001, the emphases shifted again, renewing the Cold War era reliance on traditional combat forces while expanding the need for more mobile combat units and special operations forces to deal with terrorists not tied to a single state.

The period that started on 11 September 2001 appears to carry forward the post-Cold War decade's emphasis on gendarme operations but with an important modification. Kenneth Anderson, a professor of international law at American University, noted that the terrorist attacks were "simultaneously an act of war and a crime." A crime committed against the almost 3,000 people who were killed and an act of war aimed at the United States. The American response, usually referred to as the "Global War on Terrorism" or GWOT, pulled together both sides of the operational tradition, a conventional war against the Taliban-dominated state of Afghanistan, which harbored the terrorists, and a worldwide manhunt for the perpetrators, their accomplices, and financiers.[1] The war against the Taliban regime was prosecuted effectively and ended quickly. However, the law enforcement operation to catch and punish the terrorists and their accomplices went on, reflecting the past record of gendarme operations as tending to be long, complex, frustrating, and frequently deadly.

The twentieth century saw an increasing tendency of gendarme operations to become global, slowly expanding and moving from enforcement of national law to international law and standards. A substantial portion of missions always dealt with situations close to the United States, in areas of traditional interest, along the southern border and in Caribbean waters, but gendarme operations increasingly took place in more remote locales as America's interests expanded and as its ability to project forces grew. In the 1990s, US operations clustered in areas removed from US interests—sub-Saharan Africa, the Balkans, and southwest Asia—borderland areas in which cultures overlapped and confronted each other and competition caused friction and war.

Some operational continuity connected the periods divided by the events of September 11, 2001. **Provide Hope**, the delivery of humanitarian aid to elements of the former USSR, started in 1992 and provided medical supplies and equipment through much of the 1990s. Together with the Joint Contact Team Program, through which American military specialists provided advice and counsel to fellow military professionals in the armed forces of former Warsaw Pact states, **Operation Provide Hope** was one of the few exceptions to the almost complete disappearance of the former Soviet Union from American operational concern. In the 500th mission of this operation, a C-5 aircraft of the 436th Airlift Wing, US Air Force, landed at Tashkent, Uzbekistan, on June 17, 1997, and delivered privately donated medicines to the local hospital.[2] Beginning two years later, Army Special Forces troops regularly went to Uzbekistan on training missions, "one element of an accelerating security arrangement in which the two nations were laying the groundwork for more extensive military cooperation." That connection continued to expand after 2000. Beginning in 1995, opportunities for Uzbek officers to study in the United States expanded, as did regular consultations between CENTCOM and the US embassy with Uzbek Ministry of Defense officials. American assistance in acquisition of supplies and equipment other than arms also increased.[3]

After the events of 9/11, American operations continued to rely on contractors and on reservists. Brown and Root, the company that carried out the huge facilities development program in the Balkans, built Camp Delta at the Guantanamo naval base for the detention of suspected terrorists. Army Reserve and National Guard military police companies provided most of the Guantanamo guard force.[4]

While the events of 9/11 ended the post-Cold War era of the 1990s, the cluster of operations against Saddam Hussein in Southwest Asia and the group of stability operations in the Balkans continued. Three long-term joint task forces also remained active. They were: **Computer Network Operations**, which was established on 1 January 1999; **Joint Task Force Civil Support** in Joint Forces Command, with its mission of preparing to cope with the effects of weapons of mass destruction or "WMD consequence management"; and **Joint Task Force Full Accounting** in Hawaii.

There had been operational responses to terrorist actions before September 11, 2001. **Desert Focus** in 1996 had followed the bombing of the military barracks at Khobar Towers in Saudi Arabia, and two operations, **Resolute Response** and **Incident Reach** in 1998, reacted to the attacks on American embassies in Africa. **Determined Response** came after the attack on the USS *Cole* in 2000. Begun after the attacks of September 11, 2001, **Operation Enduring Freedom** was an operational campaign in the Global War on Terrorism, and **Operation Noble Eagle** focused on protecting the United States from terrorist attacks. A variety of activities designed to train and equip the military forces of the Philippines, Georgia, and Yemen for counter-terrorist operations were begun. Designed to build working relationships and rapport between American Special Operations Forces and their foreign counterparts, these programs had their roots in the period before the 2001 attacks.[5]

By the turn of the twenty-first century, before counter-terrorism became the focus of interest, Department of Defense involvement in counter-drug operations was declining. Priorities changed, funding decreased, and emphasis shifted toward other areas, among them peacekeeping and training. After September 2001, the trend continued.[6] The effort to control and reduce the flow of drugs into the United States did presage the new Global War On Terrorism in its effort to bring to justice law breakers operating in locations far from the United States and in its effort to deal with stateless transnational enemies, drug cartels rather than organized terrorist groups. Both counter-drug and counter-terrorist efforts operated simultaneously in widely separated places, drew on the assets of several combatant commands, used the metaphor of "war" to describe far-flung gendarme operations, and seem destined for long, indeterminate battles against shadowy foes.

Both the drug war and the campaign to bring terrorists to justice resembled the long campaigns in the Balkans and against Saddam Hussein in one important respect. All were single, long-term campaigns in which individual operations varied greatly and had the characteristics of contingencies. Within the long-range context of the campaign itself, these operations were often brief and extemporaneous, and were dissimilar. They also took place in numerous locations and involved the full range of gendarme operations—peacekeeping, disaster relief and other humanitarian assistance, law enforcement, and even nation building. However, appreciation of the broader context of the individual operations differed widely. In the case of the campaign in the Balkans and the one focused on Iraq, the sense of an overall long-term enterprise never seemed to emerge. While for the so-called drug war, such an awareness developed in Southern Command but did not extend to the other military participants and contributors. In the campaign against the terrorists who struck the United States and their supporters, such an understanding seems to have informed the effort from its earliest stages. As with the "wars" on drugs, crime, and poverty, the war on terrorism did not appear to promise a clear and decisive triumph in the near-term.[7]

Endnotes

Preface:

1. Gerald H. Turley, "Prepare for the Most Likely Commitments," *Proceedings of the US Naval Institute* (April 2001), p. 89.

2. "Verbatim," *Washington Post*, 16 July 2000, p. B2.

Chapter 1

1. "Stability operations are typically characterized by intra-state conflict between two or more factions divided over issues such as ethnicity, nationality and religion. A stability operation is an umbrella term encompassing peace building, peacekeeping, peacemaking and peace enforcement." Catherine Abbott, "Utilization of New Zealand Defence Force Capabilities on International Stability and Military Operations 1946-1998," Unpublished mss, p. 4. Not all observers see these operations as existing on a continuum. Some view peace enforcement as categorically different from peacekeeping, because the former requires participants to be heavily armed, involves much greater danger, and carries a much higher likelihood that the arms will be used. *See* Frederick Fleitz, *Peacekeeping Fiascoes of the 1990s: Causes, Solutions, and US Interests* (Westport, CT: Praeger, 2002).

2. At the end of November 2002, the author was able to identify 450 operational names; some were used only for planning purposes; others cross-referenced to other names. Nevertheless, the large number of names is confusing. The more extensive list of names published in William M. Arkin, *Code Names: Deciphering US Military Plans, Programs and Operations in the 9/11 World* (Hanover, NH: Steerforth Press, 2004) also includes names of exercises and programs.

3. On the naming of operations, both the theory, with its well-ordered system based on blocs of letters assigned to the combatant commands, and the practice, with its eye to the public image, *see* the following: Chairman of the Joint Chiefs of Staff Manual 3150.29A, "Code Word, Nickname, and Exercise Term Report (Short Title—NIC-

KA), April 23, 1998; Linton Weeks, "Operation War Language: How the Pentagon Mints its Campaign Monikers," *Washington Post*, September 21, 2001, p. C1; Gregory C. Sieminski, "The Art of Naming Operations," Naval War College student paper, in author's files.

4. Data was assembled by the author from a variety of Joint Staff sources.

5. *See* Richard N. Haass, *Intervention: The Use of American Military Force in the Post-Cold War World* (Washington, DC: The Brookings Institution, 1994), p. 3.

6. Thomas Mockaitis, "From Counterinsurgency to Peace Enforcement," *Peace Operations Between War and Peace*, edited by Erwin A. Schmidl (London: Frank Cass, 2000), pp. 42-43.

7. US Army, *FM 100-23: Peace Operations* (Washington, DC: Headquarters, Department of the Army, 1994), p. iii.

8. Peter Walker and Jonathan Walter, eds., *World Disasters Report 2000: Focus on Public Health* (Geneva: International Federation of Red Cross and Red Crescent Societies, 2000), pp. 159-162. The database contains information from a variety of sources, and the Red Cross considers its overall compilation "relative and indicative, rather than absolute." "Priority is given to data from UN agencies, followed by OFDA, and then governments and the International Federation. The priority is not a reflection of the quality or value of the data, but it recognizes that most reporting sources do not cover all disasters or have political limitations that may affect the figures."

9. Karin Von Hippel, *Democracy by Force: US Military Intervention in the Post-Cold War World* (New York: Cambridge University Press, 2000) pp. 2-3.

10. Andrew J. Birtle, *US Army Counterinsurgency and Contingency Operations Doctrine, 1860-1941* (Washington, DC: US Army Center of Military History, 1998), p. 3.

11. Ibid.

12. Ibid.

Chapter 2

1. *See* Edward M. Coffman, "The Duality of the American Military Tradition," *Journal of Military History* 64 (October 2000), pp. 967-980, and the works cited in Coffman's article regarding the history of reserve components of United States forces.

2. *See*, for example, Marvin A. Kreidberg and Merton G. Henry, *History of Military Mobilization in the United States Army, 1775-1945* (Washington, DC: Department of the Army, 1955).

3. Von Hippel, *Democracy by Force*, p. 177, characterizes the United States military's view of peace support operations as persistent "isolationist policy and antipathy ...."

4. James A. Schear, "The Interagency Planning Process," Interagency Coordination and Planning Seminar, National Foreign Affairs Training Center, October 11, 2000.

5. Remarks of George W. Bush, transcript of presidential debate of October 11, 2000, *New York Times*, October 12, 2000, pp. A20-21. *See also* Andrea Stone, "Let Others Take Up Peacekeeping, Pentagon's No. 2 Says," *USA Today*, June 19, 2001.

6. Birtle, *US Army Counterinsurgency and Contingency Operations Doctrine*, p. 4.

7. Roy W. Davies, *Service in the Roman Army*, David Breeze and Valerie A. Maxfield, eds. (New York: Columbia University Press, 1989), p. 34. On the Roman army's role in protecting and nurturing society on various frontiers, *see*: Stephen K. Drummond, "The Roman Army as a Frontier Institution in the First and Second Centuries AD," unpublished doctoral dissertation, University of Kansas, 1981; Yann Le Bohec, *The Imperial Roman Army*, Raphael Bate trans., (London: Routledge, 1994); Derek Williams, *Romans and Barbarians: Four Views from the Empire's Edge, 1*ˢᵗ *Century AD* (New York: St. Martin's Press, 1998); Derek Williams, *The Reach of Rome: A History of the Roman Imperial Frontier 1*ˢᵗ*-5*ᵇ *Centuries AD* (New York: St. Martin's Press, 1996).

8. Williams, *Reach of Rome*, p. 38.

9. Michael L. Tate, *The Frontier Army and the Settlement of the West* (Norman: University of Oklahoma Press, 1999), p. x; Stephen K. Drummond, "The Roman Army as a Frontier Institution in the First and Second Centuries AD," unpublished doctoral dissertation, University of Kansas, 1981, p. 157. Roman tactics and equipment were designed to reduce their casualties. As Robert Kaplan noted, "We are not the first great empire to despise casualties." Robert D. Kaplan, *Warrior Politics: Why Leadership Demands a Pagan Ethos* (New York: Random House, 2002), pp. 123-124.

10. Coffman, "The Duality of the American Military Tradition," pp. 971-972.

11. Alvin M. Josephy, Jr., *The Indian Heritage of America* (New York: Alfred A. Knopf, 1970), p. 316; Allan R. Millett and Peter Maslowski, *For the Common Defense: A Military History of the United States of America* (New York: Macmillan, 1984), p. 92; William H. Guthman, *March to Massacre: A History of the First Seven Years of the United States Army* (New York: McGraw-Hill Book Company, 1975), pp. 220-244; Robert M. Utley, "The Contribution of the Frontier to the American Military Tradition," in *The Harmon Memorial Lectures in Military History, 1959-1987*, edited by Harry R. Borowski, (Washington, DC: Office of Air Force History, 1988), p. 533. The Continental Army had been disbanded in 1784, and a single regiment, the 1ˢᵗ American Regiment, was established immediately afterward. This unit depended on the states for manpower and Congress for money. The first units of a truly national army were not established until the creation of General "Mad Anthony" Wayne's Legion of the United States, over 5,000 strong, in 1793. *See* Millett and Maslowski, *Common Defense*, pp. 86-93.

12. John B. Wilson, *Campaign Streamers of the United States Army* (Washington, DC: The Institute of Land Warfare, 1995), p. 16.

13. Walter Millis, *Arms and Men: A Study in American Military History* (New York: G. P. Putnam's Sons, 1956), p. 110; Birtle, *US Army Counterinsurgency*, p. 7; Utley, "The Contribution of the Frontier to the American Military Tradition," p. 527. For a detailed discussion of the missions summarized by Utley, *see* Tate, *Frontier Army*.

14. Kenneth J. Hagan, *This People's Navy: The Making of American Sea Power* (New York: The Free Press, 1991), pp. 157-158. *Also see* Frank N.

Schubert, ed., *The Nation Builders: A Sesquicenten-nial History of the Corps of Topographical Engineers 1838-1863* (Fort Belvoir, VA: Office of History, US Army Corps of Engineers, 1988); Frank N. Schubert, *Vanguard of Expansion: Army Engineers in the Trans-Mississippi West 1819-1879* (Washington, DC: Historical Division, Office of the Chief of Engineers, 1980).

15. *See* Jack Sweetman, *American Naval History: An Illustrated Chronology of the US Navy and Marine Corps, 1775-Present* (Annapolis: Naval Institute Press, 1989), passim for the Navy's operational history in this period.

16. Hagan, *This People's Navy*, p. 94.

17. Sweetman, *American Naval History*, pp. 39-49, 61; Ellen C. Collier, *Instances of Use of United States Armed Forces Abroad, 1798-1989* (Washington, DC: Congressional Research Service report No. 89-651 F, 1989), p. 4; Hagan, *This People's Navy*, p. 92. An 1820 American law defined the slave trade as piracy.

18. Paul Kennedy, *The Rise and Fall of the Great Powers* (New York: Random House, 1987), pp. 154-155; Max Boot, *The Savage Wars of Peace: Small Wars and the Rise of American Power* (New York: Basic Books, 2002), p. 51. *Also see* Millis, *Arms and Men*, p. 85.

19. Birtle, *US Army Counterinsurgency and Contingency Operations Doctrine*, p. 4; Boot, *Savage Wars*, p. 39.

20. "The shift from slavery to freedom precipitated by the Civil War was the cataclysmic event and central dilemma of the [nineteenth] century." Kirk Savage, *Standing Soldiers, Kneeling Slaves: Race, War, and Monument in Nineteenth-Century America* (Princeton, New Jersey: Princeton University Press, 1997), p. 3. Nevertheless, it is also true that the war with Mexico was "the only formally declared American war fought between 1815 and 1898." Hagan, *This People's Navy*, p. 124.

21. Birtle, *US Army Counterinsurgency and Contingency Operations Doctrine*, p. 5.

22. United States Army, *Record of Engagements with Hostile Indians within the Military Division of the Missouri from 1868 to 1882, Lieutenant General P. H. Sheridan, Commanding* (Washington, DC: Government Printing Office, 1882), pp. 7-102.

23. Three separate counts yield anywhere from 939 to 1,282. A composite count of all encounters listed in at least one of these three sources totals 1,296. *See*: Adjutant General's Office, *Chronological List of Actions, &c., With Indians, From January 1, 1866, to January, 1891*; Francis E. Heitman, *Historical Register and Dictionary of the United States Army, from its Organization, September 29, 1789, to March 2, 1903*, vol. 2 (Washington: Government Printing Office, 1903), pp. 426-449; George W. Webb, *Chronological List of Engagements Between the Regular Army of the United States and Various Tribes of Hostile Indians Which Occurred During the Years 1790 to 1898, Inclusive* (St. Joseph, MO: National Indian War Veterans, 1939). A fourth count was made by Thomas D. Phillips, "The Black Regulars," in *The West of the American People*, edited by Allan G. Bogue, Thomas D. Phillips, and James E. Wright (Itasca, IL: F. E. Peacock Publishers, Inc., n.d.), p. 141. Phillips concluded that there had been 2,704 armed encounters but neither published a list nor explained his research.

24. Wilson, *Campaign Streamers*, p. 16; John M. Carroll, *The Indian Wars Campaign Medal: Its History and Its Recipients* (Mattituck, NY: J. M. Carroll & Co., 1992), p. iii.

25. John M. Gates, "Indians and Insurrectos," p. 4, in Gates, *The US Army in Irregular Warfare* (http://www.wooster.edu/history/jgates/book-ch2.html (copy in author's files). *Also see* Gerald F. Linderman, *The Mirror of War: American Society and the Spanish-American War* (Ann Arbor: University of Michigan Press, 1974), p. 61.

26. John Bigelow, "Tenth Regiment of Cavalry," *Journal of the Military Service Institution* 8 (March 1892), p. 221.

27. George Andrews, "Twenty-fifth Regiment of Infantry," *Journal of the Military Service Institution* 8 (March 1892), p. 225.

28. Quoted in Edward T. Lininthal, *Sacred Ground: Americans and their Battlefields* (Urbana: University of Illinois Press, 1991), p. 131.

29. Utley, "The Contribution of the Frontier to the American Military Tradition," p. 530.

30. Quoted in Perry D. Jamieson, *Crossing the Deadly Ground: United States Army Tactics, 1865-1899* (Tuscaloosa: University of Alabama Press, 1994), pp. 120-121.

31. Boot, *Savage Wars of Peace*, p. 283. A consequence of preoccupation with large conventional warfare was that there was little written on the conduct of frontier wars. Edward S. Farrow, *Mountain Scouting, A Handbook for Officers and Soldiers on the Frontier* (New York: E. S. Farrow, 1881), was, according to historian Jerome A. Greene, "something of a phenomenon, for treatises dealing with the formal methodology of Indian warfare are virtually nonexistent." *See* Greene, "Introduction," Farrow, *Mountain Scouting*, p. 3. Farrow was an experienced frontier officer, cited for bravery in action during the Nez Percé War of 1879, who taught tactics at the Military Academy. On the overall matter of the transmission of lessons learned in the field during the hard years of frontier combat against the western tribes, *see* Thomas A. Dowling, "Intelligence in the Final Indian Wars, 1866-1887" (MA thesis, Joint Military Intelligence College, 1996).

32. Jerome A. Greene, "Foreword," Farrow, *Mountain Scouting*, p. 3. Greene's essay provides a good summary of the Army's tactical approach to battle with western tribes.

33. Richard H. Shultz, Jr., *In the Aftermath of War: US Support for Reconstruction and Nation-Building in Panama Following Just Cause* (Maxwell Air Force Base, AL: Air University Press, 1993), p. 19.

34. Institute for Foreign Policy Analysis, *Summary Report of a Conference On: Operations Other Than War* (Washington: IFPA, 1995), p. v.

35. Tate, *Frontier Army*, p. 216.

36. Tate, *Frontier Army*, p. 215.

37. Tate, *Frontier Army*, pp. 215-216.

38. James E. Sefton, *The United States Army and Reconstruction 1865-1877* (Baton Rouge: Louisiana State University Press, 1967), p. 41.

39. For a copy of the pertinent section of the 1879 Appropriations Act (Section 1385, Chapter LXVII, Title 18, US Code), *see* William W. Epley, comp., *Roles and Missions of the United States Army: Basic Documents with Annotations and Bibliography* (Washington, DC: US Army Center of Military History, 1991), p. 119. For many years, historians accepted the Southern white view that this Act was adopted in response to excesses and abuses of power by the military. That view survives in Epley, *Roles and Missions*, and in another official Army

volume, Clayton D. Laurie and Ronald H. Cole, *The Role of Federal Military Forces in Domestic Disorders 1877-1945*, (Washington, DC: US Army Center of Military History, 1997). For more balanced perspectives, *see* Robert W. Coakley, *The Role of Federal Military Forces in Domestic Disorders 1789-1878*, (Washington, DC: US Army Center of Military History, 1988), and Sefton, *United States Army and Reconstruction*.

40. Tate, *Frontier Army*, pp. 98-99, 107-109.

41. Frank N. Schubert, *Buffalo Soldiers, Braves and the Brass: the Story of Fort Robinson, Nebraska* (Shippensburg, PA: White Mane Publishing Company, 1993), p. 121.

42. Many of these operations are mentioned in Tate, *Frontier Army*, pp. 216-225. *Also see* Gaines M. Foster, *The Demands of Humanity: Army Medical Disaster Relief* (Washington, DC: Center of Military History, 1983); Jerry M. Cooper, "The Army and Industrial Workers: Strikebreaking in the Late Nineteenth Century," *Soldiers and Civilians: the US Army and the American People*, edited by Garry D. Ryan and Timothy K. Nenninger (Washington, DC: National Archives and Records Administration, 1987); Clayton D. Laurie, "Extinguishing Frontier Brushfires: The US Army's Role in Quelling the Pullman Strike in the West, 1894," *Journal of the West* 32 (April 1993), pp. 54-63; Laurie and Cole, *The Role of Federal Military Forces.*

43. Utley, "The Contribution of the Frontier to the American Military Tradition," p. 530.

44. Sweetman, *American Naval History*, pp. 91-102; Collier, *Instances of Use of United States Armed Forces Abroad, 1798-1989*, pp. 6-8.

45. Henry H. Shelton, "Peace Operations: The Forces Required," *National Security Studies Quarterly* 6 (Summer 2000), p. 105.

Chapter 3

1. Sweetman, *American Naval History*, pp. 116-154; Collier, *Instances of Use of United States Armed Forces Abroad, 1798-1989*, pp. 9-14; John Whiteclay Chambers II, editor, *The Oxford Companion to American Military History* (New York: Oxford University Press, 1999), pp. 98, 580.

2. Hagan, *This People's Navy*, pp. 236-237.

3. Lester D. Langley, *The Banana Wars: United States Intervention in the Caribbean, 1898-1934* (Wilmington, DE: Scholarly Resources, 2002), p. 39; Maurice Matloff, ed., *American Military History* (Washington, DC: US Army Center of Military History, 1989), pp. 352-353, 355; Millett and Maslowski, *For the Common Defense*, pp. 318-319.

4. The United States never joined the League of Nations, but concern for maintenance of some semblance of stability in Latin America demanded that some commitment be made to this effort to avert war over the small Amazon River port of Leticia. *See* William O. Scroggs, *The United States in World Affairs: An Account of American Foreign Relations, 1933* (New York: Harper & Brothers for the Council on Foreign Relations, 1934); p. 193.

5. Sweetman, *American Naval History*, pp. 119, 120, 127, 146, 147, 156; Norman Polmar, *Aircraft Carriers: A History of Carrier Aviation and Its Influence on World Events* (Garden City, NY: Doubleday, 1969), p. 52. The largest American humanitarian operation of all time did not involve American forces in a management role. The American Relief Administration in 1921-1922 fed more than ten million Russian adults and children during 1921-1922. This remarkable operation involved 199 Americans assisted by about 120,000 Soviets. *See* Bertrand M. Patenaude, *The Big Show in Bololand: The American Relief Expedition to Soviet Russia in the Famine of 1921* (Stanford: Stanford University Press, 2002).

6. Walker and Walter, eds., *World Disasters Report 2000*, p. 176.

7. Kenneth Anderson, "Language, Law and Terror," (London) *Times Literary Supplement*, no. 5138 (September 21, 2001), pp. 13-15.

8. Tate, *Frontier Army*, pp. 108-110.

9. For an overview of early projects of these two types, *see* Schubert, ed., *The Nation Builders*.

10. *See* John M. Gates, *Schoolbooks and Krags: The US Army in the Philippines, 1898-1902* (Westport, CT: Greenwood Press, 1973); Hans Schmidt, *The United States Occupation of Haiti, 1915-1934* (New Brunswick, NJ: Rutgers University Press, 1971); Bruce J. Calder, *The Impact of Intervention: The Dominican Republic During the US Occupation of 1916-1924* (Austin: University of Texas Press, 1984); Stephen M. Fuller and Graham A.

Cosmas, *Marines in the Dominican Republic 1916-1924* (Washington, DC: History and Museums Division, Headquarters, US Marine Corps, 1974); Neill Macaulay, *The Sandino Affair* (Durham, NC: Duke University Press, 1985); and Allan R. Millett, *Semper Fidelis: The History of the United States Marine Corps* (New York: The Free Press, 1991).

11. Quoted in John S. D. Eisenhower, *Intervention! The United States and the Mexican Revolution 1913-1917* (New York: W. W. Norton & Company, 1993), p. 32.

12. David A. Wilson, "Nation-Building and Revolutionary War," in Karl W. Deutsch and William J. Foltz, eds., *Nation-Building* (New York: Atherton Press, 1966), p. 84.

13. This definition very closely follows that proposed by Von Hippel, *Democracy by Force*, p. 10. *Also see* Haass, *Intervention*, p. 61.

14. Von Hippel, *Democracy by Force*, p. 175.

15. *See* Robert T. Cossaboom, *The Joint Contact Team Program* (Washington, DC: Joint History Office, Office of the Chairman of the Joint Chiefs of Staff, 1997).

16. Institute for Foreign Policy Analysis, *Summary Report of a Conference on: Operations Other Than War*, p. 5.

17. 10 *US Code Annotated* 401 (1998), paragraphs (c)(3), (e)(2), and (e)(4).

18. Edward Luttwak, "A Post-Heroic Military Policy," *Foreign Affairs* 75 (June-August 1996), p. 33. Rudolph Vecoli described the international consensus that held together so-called free-world states and stifled the outbreak of small conflicts not related to the great superpower competition as "the discipline of fear ...." Vecoli, "American Centrifuge: Ethnicity in the United States at the End of the Century," *Politics and Progress: American Society and the State since 1865*, Andrew E. Kersten and Kriste Lindenmeyer, eds. (Westport, CT: Praeger, 2001), p. 140.

19. Shultz, *In the Aftermath of War*, p. 19; Barry M. Blechman and Stephen S. Kaplan, *Force Without War: US Armed Forces as a Political Instrument* (Washington DC: Brookings Institution, 1978), p. 23; Gerald H. Turley, "Prepare for the Most Likely Commitments," *Proceedings of the US Naval Institute (April, 2001)*, pp. 88-89; Conrad C. Crane,

Avoiding Vietnam: The US Army's Response to Defeat in Southeast Asia (Carlisle, PA: US Army Strategic Studies Institute, 2002), p. 2.

20. Turley, "Prepare for the Most Likely Commitments," pp. 88-89.

21. Charles W. Gwynn, *Imperial Policing*, (London: Macmillan and Co., Ltd., 1934, 1939), p. 7.

22. Taylor Branch, *Parting the Waters: America in the King Years, 1954-1963* (New York: Simon and Schuster, 1988), p. 670; William Doyle, *An American Insurrection: the Battle of Oxford, Mississippi, 1962* (New York: Doubleday, 2001), pp. 277-278. For a summary of earlier uses of Federal armed forces to suppress civil disturbances, *see* Doyle, *An American Insurrection*, pp. 101-102. The quotation is from Doyle, *An American Insurrection*, p. 257.

23. Both the lists and the quoted phrase are in Yahya Sadowski, *The Myth of Global Chaos* (Washington, DC: The Brookings Institution Press, 1998), pp. 178-179.

24. Sadowski, *The Myth of Global Chaos*, p. 84.

25. Clive Emsley, *Gendarmes and the State in Nineteenth Century Europe* (New York: Oxford University Press, 1999), pp. 7-8, 17, 149-152. The quotation is from page 7.

26. The US Army also had substantial experience with domestic intelligence gathering. The Army became prominent in domestic surveillance directed against American citizens during World War I, when "Army intelligence ... became a vast force at home for the first time in history," and remained active through the Depression, World War II, and into the Cold War. This role became especially controversial because of "massive army surveillance of dissenters" during the Vietnam War years, but by then domestic military intelligence activities had a long history, starting as unorganized and extemporaneous in the nineteenth century and becoming more systematic in the twentieth. *See* Joan M. Jensen, *Army Surveillance in America, 1775-1980* (New Haven: Yale University Press, 1991). The quotations are from pages 177 and 230.

27. Emsley, *Gendarmes and the State*, pp. 154-155, 172, 204-205.

28. Thomas R. Mockaitis, *British Counterinsurgency, 1919-1960* (New York: St. Martin's Press, 1990), p. 163.

29. The names of two of the chapters in Birtle, *US Army Counterinsurgency and Contingency Operations Doctrine* reflect the importance of this type of operation. Chapter 3, "The Constabulary Years, 1865-1898," covered operations during Reconstruction in the South and against Indians in the West. Chapter 5, "The Imperial Constabulary Years, 1900-1913," covered missions in China, Cuba, and the Philippines.

30. David Robertson, "Modern Technology and the Future of the Soldier," *Europe's New Security Challenges,* Heinz Gärtner, Adrian Hyde-Price and Erich Reiter, eds. (Boulder, CO: Lynne Rienner, 2001), p. 81. The requirement to fight and win two "major theater wars" was reminiscent of the approach of another unrivalled superpower, Great Britain in the 1880s. The huge shipbuilding program of 1884 was justified by a "two-power standard," meaning that "the Royal Navy ought always to be equal or superior to the combined forces of the next two largest navies in the world." William H. McNeill, *The Pursuit of Power: Technology, Armed Force, and Society Since AD 1000* (Chicago: University of Chicago Press, 1982), pp. 274-275.

31. *See,* for example, Institute for Foreign Policy Analysis, *Summary Report of a Conference on: Operations Other Than War,* for expressions of an Army consensus in favor of avoiding involvement in gendarme operations.

32. Lars-Erik Nelson, "Armed to the Teeth," *New York Daily News*, 3 September 2000, DL Washington.

33. Utley, *The Contribution of the Frontier to the American Military Tradition*, p. 528.

34. Eliot A. Cohen, "Defending America in the Twenty-first Century," *Foreign Affairs* 79 (November-December 2000), p. 46.

35. Richard C. Hottelet, "Moving Beyond Makeshift Peacekeeping," *Christian Science Monitor*, 27 Sep 2000, p. 11.

36. James Kitfield, "Standing Apart," *National Journal*, June 13, 1998.

Chapter 4

1. *Savannah* (Georgia) *Morning News*, July 29, 2001; Timothy J. Dunn, *The Militarization of the US-Mexican Border, 1872-1992: Low-Intensity*

Conflict Comes Home (Austin: The Center for Mexican American Studies, The University of Texas at Austin, 1996), pp. 2-3, 25; National Defense Authorization Act for Fiscal Year 1989, Public Law 100-456, 29 September 1988 (102 Stat. 1918). Dunn argues that the expanded use of the military services in counter-drug operations on the border and military involvement in coordination of efforts to stem illegal immigration indicate an increasing militarization of the border with Mexico. *See* Dunn, *Militarization of the US-Mexican Border*, pp. 133-138.

2. To their credit, military officers almost immediately began thinking and writing about aspects of their role in counter-drug missions. Five of the seven articles in the March 1990 issue of *Military Review*, published by the Army's Command and General Staff College, dealt with matters related to operations against drug traffickers. The *Proceedings of the US Naval Institute* also had three articles on the subject during the first half of 1990, one article was about the US Coast Guard.

3. Dunn, *Militarization of the US-Mexican Border*, p. 25; US General Accounting Office, Assets DOD Contributes to Reducing the Illegal Drug Supply Have Declined (Report No. GAO/NSIAD 00-9, December 1999), p. 8; *Savannah* (Georgia) *Morning News*, July 29, 2001.

4. Sweetman, *American Naval History*, p. 145.

5. *See* Eric S. Ensign, *Intelligence in the Rum War at Sea, 1920-1933* (Washington: Joint Military Intelligence College, 2001).

6. On the planning and execution of Just Cause, see Ronald H. Cole, *Operation Just Cause: Panama* (Washington, DC: Joint History Office, 1995).

7. Other names associated with Just Cause included Blue Spoon, JTF South, Nimble Lion, and Poplar Tree.

8. Other names associated with Promote Liberty were Backstop, Hawk, Joint Task Force Panama 90, and Overwatch.

9. Adam Wolfson, "How to Think about Humanitarian War," *Commentary* 110 (July-August 2000), p. 45.

10. Other names associated with this operation were Maintain Democracy, Haiti Assistance Group (HAG), JTF Raleigh, Phoenix Halibut,

Phoenix Shark, Restore Democracy, Support Democracy, and UNMIH (United Nations Mission in Haiti).

11. *Public Papers of the Presidents of the United States: William J. Clinton, 1994*, vol. II, August 1 to December 31, 1994 (Washington, DC: GPO, 1994), p. 1572.

12. John Pitts, *Migrant Resettlement Operations*. Supplement Nr. 2 to US Southern Command History for 1 January 1994-31 December 1995 (Miami, FL: Office of the Command Historian, 1998) p. 1.

13. *See*, for example, John Pitts, *United States Southern Command, Command History: Tenure of General Barry R. McCaffrey, February 1994-February 1996* (Miami, FL: Office of the Command Historian, 1998), p. 128.

14. Pitts, *Migrant Resettlement Operations*, pp. 1-2.

15. Haass, *Intervention*, p. 47. The population of Haiti was estimated in 1982 at just over five million.

16. Pitts, *Migrant Resettlement Operations*, p. 4.

17. William S. Cohen, *Report to Congress on US Military Involvement in Major Smaller-Scale Contingencies Since the Persian Gulf War* (Washington: OSD, March 1999), pp. 13-14.

18. The Commission on America's National Interests, *America's National Interests*, July 2000, p. 37., http://www.nixoncenter.org/publications/monographs/nationalinterests.pdf.

19. Pitts, *Migrant Resettlement Operations*, pp. 1, 2, 4.

20. These were Operations Central Haven (Belize), Island Haven (Honduras), and West Haven (Costa Rica).

21. Daniel L. Haulman, *The United States Air Force and Humanitarian Airlift Operations 1947-1994* (Washington, DC: Air Force History and Museums Program, 1998), p.7.

22. *Washington Post*, January 27, 2000; *New York Times*, October 20 and 27, 2000. For an account of the lengths to which people are willing to go and the risks and deprivations that they will endure, *see* David Finkel, "Dreams Dashed on the Rocks," *Washington Post*, June 10, 2001. *Also see* Brian Lavery, "Irish Say Refugees Were in Box Aboard

Ship for Up to 8 Days," *New York Times*, December 10, 2001; John W. Fountain with Jim Yardley, "Skeletons Tell Tale of Gamble By Immigrants," *New York Times*, October 16, 2002.

23. Barbara Crosette, "Stiffer Rules Are a Threat to Refugees, Agency Says," *New York Times*, December 13, 1998; Crossette, "For Lack of Support, UN Agency Shrinks Aid to Refugees," *New York Times*, April 29, 2001; RAN, *Australian Maritime Doctrine*, p. 57; "Afghan Refugees Arrive at Anauru," *New York Times*, 19 September 2001; International Red Cross and Red Crescent Societies, *World Disasters Report 1996*, p. 78. The United States and several other major donors reduced their contributions to the UN High Commissioner which in the spring of 2001 forced the UN to cut its assistance to the estimated 22 million refugees in the world.

24. Robert Gilpin, *Global Political Economy: Understanding the International Economic Order* (Princeton, NJ: Princeton University Press, 2001), pp. 365-366. Throughout the period, the discussion of the international movements of people focused on limiting such movements.

25. International Federation of Red Cross and Red Crescent Societies, *World Disasters Report, 1996*, pp. 78, 122; Von Hippel, *Democracy By Force*, p. 170.

26. Alexander M. Monroe, *US Atlantic Command Support of Counterdrug Operations in the Caribbean 1989-1997*, p. 17. See Section 4205 of Public Law 100-690 (102 Stat. 4268) and Section 1101 of Public Law 100-456 (102 Stat. 1918).

27. David Passage, "Latin America: The Next Quarter-Century Challenges and Opportunities," in *Roles and Missions of SOF in the Aftermath of the Cold War*, edited by Richard H. Shultz, Jr., Robert L. Pfaltzgraff, Jr., and W. Bradley Stock (N.P.: n.p.), pp. 125-126.

28. US General Accounting Office, *Assets DOD Contributes to Reducing the Illegal Drug Supply Have Declined*, pp. 13-16.

29. Command History Division, United States Pacific Command, *Commander in Chief US Pacific Command History, 1990*, vol. I (Camp H. M. Smith, Hawaii, 1991), p. 90.

30. Mervin W. Stark, *US Army Forces Command Annual Command History, 1 January 1996-31*

December 1996 (Fort McPherson, GA: Military History Office, US Army Forces Command), [1998].

31. US General Accounting Office, *Assets DOD Contributes to Reducing the Illegal Drug Supply Have Declined*, p. 8. For an unclassified Joint Interagency Task Force East organization chart, see (S-NF) Monroe, *US Atlantic Command Support of Counterdrug Operations in the Caribbean 1989-1997*, p. 23; (U) "JIATF East Mission and History (JIATF-E History 20000826.doc), in (S) HQ USSOUTHCOM Historical Archives, September 1997-September 2000, disk 5.

32. Dunn, *The Militarization of the US-Mexico Border*, p. 135; Dallas Morning News, November 19, 1999.

33. This summary of counter-drug operations was compiled from annual histories of the unified commands and is understated. There tends to be a lag of a few years before histories of operations in specific years are completed. When the histories of the commands at the end of the decade are completed, they will almost certainly contain additional entries. Reported operations for Joint Task Force 6 included many activities too small for inclusion in annual histories, but they do suggest the problems in counting operations and comparing types of operations quantitatively.

34. US General Accounting Office, *Assets DOD Contributes to Reducing the Illegal Drug Supply Have Declined*, pp. 32-33; e-mail message, John Pitts, SOUTHCOM historian, to author, 6 January 2001, author's files.

35. US General Accounting Office, *Drug Control: DOD Allocates Fewer Assets to Drug Control Efforts*, (Report No. GAO/NSIAD 00-77, January 2000), pp. 1-16.

36. The number "207" is significantly smaller than the number of names of operations and was reached by counting only the names that were attached to overall missions, rather than to subsumed component command missions. For example, Joint Guard was counted as an operation, but Decisive Guard, Deliberate Guard, and Determined Guard, all of which were components of Joint Guard, were not.

37. *Report of the Quadrennial Defense Review*, May 1997, p. 4.

38. Benjamin Miller, "The Logic of US Military Interventions in the post-Cold War Era," *Contemporary Security Policy*, 19 Dec 1998, p. 81.

Chapter 5

1. Frank J. Cook, III, Jeffrey A. McChesney, Gary R. Stephens, Gregory G. Wilmoth, and William M. Wilson, *The Defense Department's Role in Humanitarian and Disaster Relief*, John F. Kennedy School of Government National Security Program Policy Analysis Paper 93-02 (Cambridge: Harvard University, 1993), pp. 2, 4.

2. The International Federation of Red Cross and Red Crescent Societies considers the category of "natural disasters" to include disasters caused by earthquakes, landslides and avalanches, epidemics, droughts, extreme temperatures, floods, forest and scrub fires, volcanoes, windstorms, insect infestations, and waves and surges. Walker and Walter, eds., *World Disasters Report 2000*, p. 172.

3. Walker and Walter, eds., *World Disasters Report 2000*, p. 169. The figure 2,468 was reached by subtracting the number of epidemics (340) and the number of non-natural disasters (2,056) from the Red Cross-Red Crescent total number of disasters (4,864).

4. *Madison* (Wisconsin) *Capital Times*, August 1, 2000; US Army Reserve Command, News Release 99-03-24; US Army Reserve Command. "Joint Task Force ?? New Horizons 99-02," briefing slides [Feb 99].

5. Billy T. Brooks and Kevin Roller, *Historical Analysis of US Military Responses: 1975-1995* (McLean, VA: Science Applications International Corporation, 1996), p. 8.

6. Ann A. Ferrante, "Chronology of the United States Marine Corps–1997," typescript (Washington, DC: US Marine Corps Historical Center).

7. Michael Chege, "What's really wrong," *Times Literary Supplement*, No. 5086 (September 22, 2000), p. 8.

8. "A Peace Strategy for Congo," *New York Times*, January 31, 2000. The comparison to the Thirty Years War has been made for another African war. *See* J. Millard Burr and Robert O. Collins, *Africa's Thirty Years War: Libya, Chad, and the Sudan, 1963-1993* (Boulder, CO: Westview Press, 1999).

9. Ian Fisher, "Can International Relief Do More Good than Harm?" *New York Times Magazine* (11 February 2001).

10. For an argument for the creation of a separate unified command dealing with Sub-Saharan Africa, *see* Richard G. Catoire, "A CINC for Sub-Saharan Africa? Rethinking the Unified Command Plan," *Parameters*, 30 (Winter 2000-2001), pp. 102-117.

11. Presidential trips are not usually considered military operations. However, they are large consumers of military resources, especially aircraft and crews, but also communications, security, and administrative assets. *See* United States Transportation Command home page: http://tacc.scott.af.mil/taccapps/custreport/MsnSummaryRpt.asp, for mission summary reports, Air Mobility Command, February 1999-July 2000. *Also see* US General Accounting Office, *Presidential Travel: Costs and Accounting for the President's 1998 Trips to Africa, Chile, and China*, GAO/NSIAD-99-164; Ellen Nakashima, "White House Travel Bill: $292 Million," *Washington Post*, August 18, 2000.

12. Atlas Response, the provision of emergency aid to flood victims in Mozambique and Madagascar, took place simultaneously with the single most expensive presidential trip to India, Bangladesh, Pakistan, Oman, and Switzerland in March 2000. The trip required 5,704 flying hours by Air Mobility Command aircraft and crews, "to ferry everything from trucks and communications equipment to the presidential limousine." By contrast, the relief effort took 1,592 hours, less than one-third of those required for the trip. Ellen Nakashima, "White House Travel Bill: $292 Million," *Washington Post*, August 18, 2000; United States Transportation Command home page: http://tacc.scott.af.mil/taccapps/custreport/MsnSummaryRpt.asp, for mission summary reports, Air Mobility Command, February 1999-July 2000.

13. David Robertson, "Modern Technology and the Future of the Soldier," *Europe's New Security Challenges*, Heinz Gärtner, Adrian Hyde-Price and Erich Reiter, eds. (Boulder, CO: Lynne Rienner, 2001), p. 71.

14. (S) E-mail, COL Jim A. Coggin, J5, to CJCS, 8 August 2000. Material quoted was unclassified. *Also see* Ian Fisher, "Congo's War Triumphs Over Peace Accord," *New York Times*, Mon, Septem-

ber 18, 2000, pp. 1, 8, DL Congo, September 13, 2000; Philip Gourevitch, "Forsaken: How a seven-nation war engulfed Congo," *New Yorker*, September 25, 2000; Michael Chege, "What's really wrong," *Times Literary Supplement*, No. 5086 (September 22, 2000), p. 8; Douglas Farah, "Upheavals Undermine Hope for W. Africa Stability," *Washington Post*, September 29, 2000, p. 29, DL Abidjan, Ivory Coast; Blaine Harden, "The US Keeps Looking for a Few Good Men," *New York Times*, August 27, 2000, *Week in Review*, pp. 1, 5; Von Hippel, *Democracy by Force*, p. 190.

15. "Security at 220 of 260 US Embassies Falls Short," *Washington Post*, September 19, 1998, p. 6.

16. Until that time the only other instance of American troops serving under UN command during the decade had been in the 1993 United Nations Protective Force (UNPROFOR) in Macedonia. This force deployed in accordance with UN Security Council Resolution 795 of 11 December 1992, to prevent escalation of ethnic clashes between Serbs and Albanians. A battalion-sized American force, called Task Force Able Sentry, joined the UNPROFOR contingent in July 1993 and participated in this organization, which numbered about 1,200, until March 1995.

17. Sadowski, *The Myth of Global Chaos*, pp. 43, 46.

18. International Federation of Red Cross and Red Crescent Societies, *World Disasters Report 1996*, p. 9.

19. International Federation of Red Cross and Red Crescent Societies, *World Disasters Report 1996*, p. 63.

20. Joseph P. Culligan, "United Nations Peace-keeping: Relations Between Civilian and Military Components," in Fariborz L. Mokhtari, ed., *Peacemaking, Peacekeeping and Coalition Warfare: The Future Role of the United Nations* (Washington, DC: National Defense University Press, 1994), pp. 57-70; US European Command, *After Action Review: Operation Support Hope 1994*, p. 2; Kenneth Allard, *Somalia Operations: Lessons Learned* (Washington, DC: NDU Press, 1995); Jonathan T. Dworken, "Restore Hope: Coordinating Relief Operations," *Joint Force Quarterly* No. 8 (Summer 1995), pp. 14-20; *Resource Guide, Unified Task Force Somalia, December 1992-May 1993, Operation Restore Hope*, (Washington, DC: US Army Center of Military History, 1994); *Joint Doctrine*

for Civil-Military Operations (Joint Publication 3-57), 8 February 2001.

21. Allard, *Somalia Operations*, pp. 69-70; Dworken, "Restore Hope: Coordinating Relief Operations," pp. 15-16. For a detailed list of Civil Military Operations Center functions, *see* Allard, *Somalia Operations*, pp. 109-111.

22. Stephen J. Guerra, *Responses to Harm's-Way and Humanitarian Situations by Naval Forces, 1990-1996*, CRM 97-100 (Alexandria, VA: Center for Naval Analyses, 1997), p. 19.

23. Daniel L. Haulman, *The United States Air Force and Humanitarian Airlift Operations 1947-1994* (Washington, DC: Air Force History and Museums Program, 1998), pp. 114-115.

24. Cook, McChesney, Stephens, Wilmoth, and Wilson, *The Defense Department's Role in Humanitarian and Disaster Relief*, p. 9.

25. *See* Table 18, Overseas Deployment, Ashore and Afloat, 1980-2000.

26. Emsley, *Gendarmes and the State in Nineteenth Century Europe*, pp. 204-207.

Chapter 6

1. Brooks and Roller, *Historical Analysis of US Military Responses: 1975-1995*, p. 32.

2. Charles C. Moskos, *The Media and the Military in Peace and Humanitarian Operations* (Chicago: McCormick Tribune Foundation, 2000), p. 8; US Agency for International Development, situation report, 17 October 1994, p. 2, mentioned 118 NGOs, but according to the Red Cross, "In Goma in 1994 … there were over 100 NGOs operating in support of refugees, while in Rwanda itself, numbers reached over 200." International Federation of Red Cross and Red Crescent Societies, *World Disasters Report 1996*, p. 63. John Keane, "Who's in charge here?" *Times Literary Supplement* (18 May 2001), p. 13, estimates that there are about 40,000 not-for-profit international nongovernmental organizations.

3. William S. Cohen, *Report of the Quadrennial Defense Review*, May 1997, p. 9. Smaller powers, including the United States in the pre-Civil War period, have usually been vocal proponents of international law and multilateral action. Great powers have relied on their power to provide

security and prosperity. The United States, while it supported multinational operations in the 1990s, remained inclined, and able, to act alone when it needed to do so. Michael Ignatief notes, "multilateral solutions to the world's problems are all very well, but they have no teeth unless America bares its fangs." *See* Robert Kagan, *Of Paradise and Power: America and Europe in the New World Order* (New York: Alfred A. Knopf, 2003), pp. 38-41, 45-46, 51-52, 75-76; Michael Ignatief, "The Burden," *New York Times Magazine*, 5 January 2003, pp. 22-27, 50, 53-54.

4. Cohen, *Report of the Quadrennial Defense Review*, May 1997, pp. 11-12.

5. Ann A. Ferrante, "Chronology of the United States Marine Corps–1999," typescript (Washington, DC: US Marine Corps Historical Center), copy in author's files. *Also see* James Kitfield, "Peacekeepers' Progress," *National Journal*, 32 (December 2000).

6. Cohen, *Report of the Quadrennial Defense Review*, May 1997, p. 12.

7. Eliot A. Cohen, "Defending America in the Twenty-first Century," *Foreign Affairs* 79 (November-December 2000), p. 45.

8. Lisa Troshinsky, "Study Changes 'Two MTW' Standard, But Lacks Measuring Tools," *Navy News & Undersea Technology*, 2 October 2000, p. 1.

9. D. Robert Worley, *Challenges to Train, Organize, and Equip the Complete Combined Arms Team: The Joint Task Force* (IDA paper P-3431, September 1998), pp. 10-12.

10. Stephen J. Guerra, *Responses to Harm's-Way and Humanitarian Situations by Naval Forces, 1990-1996,* CRM 97-100, (Alexandria VA: Center for Naval Analyses, 1997), p. 26.

11. Henry H. Gaffney, Jr., Eugene Cobble, Dmitry Gorenburg, Adam Moody, Richard Weitz, and Daniel Whiteneck, *US Navy Responses to Situations, 1970-1999* (Alexandria, VA: Center for Naval Analyses, 2000), pp. 63, 77. This essay on the 1990s shows some understanding of how the operations of the decade make sense as clusters. The authors perceive the clusters somewhat differently, adding Haiti and Somalia to the two emphasized in this essay. They attached greater importance to the two clusters of naval operations in the Arabian Gulf and the Adriatic Sea, arguing

that these two fueled the perception of response 'overload,' given their duration, the routine nature of follow-on operations, and in the case of the Gulf, the scheduling demands imposed by the great transit distances to that area, p. 79.

12. The war in Vietnam also saw a proliferation of operational names, about twenty English-language names per year in the late 1960s, but there was never any question that they were all components of a single large conflict. For a chronology that identifies the many operations, *see* James S. Olson ed., *Dictionary of the Vietnam War* (Westport, CT: Greenwood Press, 1988), pp. 547-560.

13. US General Accounting Office, *Defense Budget: Fiscal Year 2000 Contingency Operations Costs and Funding*, GAO/NSAID-00-168, pp. 2-3. Between October 1994, when the number of people involved first reached into the thousands, until October 2000, the number deployed as of early October of every year are: 5,826 (1994), 4500 (1995), 23,946 (1996), 17,659 (1997), 11,981 (1998), 14,979 (1999), and 13,082 (2000).

14. The eight were: Vigilant Warrior, Vigilant Sentinel, Desert Thunder, Desert Fox, Desert Strike, Provide Comfort, Northern Watch, and Southern Watch.

15. "Overall, the United States usually maintains about 20,000 military personnel in the region [Southwest Asia], at a cost of at least $1.5 billion a year." Thomas E. Ricks, "Persian Gulf, US Danger Zone," *Washington Post*, Sunday, 15 October 2000, pp. A1, A23; US General Accounting Office, *Defense Budget: Fiscal Year 2000 Contingency Operations Costs and Funding*, p. 3.

16. *See,* for example, *Dallas Morning News*, 9 October 2000, regarding Air National Guard units from California, Oklahoma, Texas, and Iowa.

17. Other names associated with this effort were Continue Hope, Quick Draw, JTF Somalia, Impressive Lift, United Nations Observer Mission in Somalia (UNOSOM) I and II, United Shield, and Phoenix Oryx.

18. There are at least three views of the Bush administration's commitment during the summer of 1992 to support the relief effort in Somalia. First, there is the view that the decision to commit aircraft for delivery of relief supplies was motivated purely by humanitarian concerns, which was the view articulated at the Bush Library during a

conference on military intervention in November, 2000. According to this perspective, President Bush was driven solely by concern for the misery in Somalia. Another view holds that the Bush administration response to Somalia was a direct response to images of starvation on television, a classic case of "the CNN effect." This is the view taken in Walter Poole's draft study, "The Effort to Save Somalia, August 1992-March 1994," (S) Joint History Office: draft manuscript, October 2000. This "CNN Effect" has a corollary, known as "the 'Do Something Effect,'" caused by increased refugee flow affecting developed countries, media attention to suffering, and the felt need to defy "nasty rulers." *See* Von Hippel, *Democracy by Force*, pp. 25-26. Finally, there is the view of Samantha Power that the humanitarian response was driven by an effort to reduce attention to images of misery in the Balkans, where the commitment required to mitigate the misery was far larger and riskier. According to Power, the initiative in Somalia succeeded in diminishing coverage and therefore, interest in the Balkan tragedy, kind of an indirect "CNN effect." Samantha Power, *"A Problem from Hell," America and the Age of Genocide* (2002), pp. 285-286.

19. Jonathan Stevenson, *Losing Mogadishu: Testing US Policy in Somalia* (Annapolis: Naval Institute Press, 1995), pp. 5, 7-9, 11-14, 43.

20. For a vivid description of the events in Mogadishu, *see* Mark Bowden, *Black Hawk Down: A Story of Modern War* (New York: Atlantic Monthly Press, 1999).

21. David Halberstam, "Clinton and the Generals," *Vanity Fair*, (September 2001).

22. Poole, "The Effort to Save Somalia, August 1992-March 1994," (S), pp. 88-92. Section cited is unclassified.

23. General Joseph P. Hoar, USMC, Commander in Chief, US Central Command, coined this term and used it in an article "A CINC's Perspective," *Joint Forces Quarterly*, Number 2, Autumn 1993, according to Jay E. Hines, "Forged in the Desert," *Desert Shield/Desert Storm: The 10ᵗʰ Anniversary of the Gulf War*, edited by Charles Oldham (Tampa, FL: Faircount, LLC, 2001), p. 61.

24. For a critique of this "normal" model, *see* Eliot A. Cohen, *Supreme Command: Soldiers, Statesmen,*

and Leadership in Wartime (New York: The Free Press, 2002).

25. Cohen, *Report of the Quadrennial Defense Review*, May 1997, pp. 8-9.

26. "Military Support to Complex Humanitarian Emergencies from Practice to Policy," 26 Oct 95, http://www.cna.org/newsevents/conferences/95cf. html (copy in author's files, JHO); *Also see* Thomas R. Mockaitis, "From Counterinsurgency to Peace Enforcement: New Names for Old Games?" in Erwin A. Schmidl, ed., *Peace Operations Between War and Peace* (London: Frank Cass, 2000), p. 54.

27. Zinni urged the importance of allowing for "... mission shift (a conscious evolution that responds to the changing situation) ...." *See* his "Military Support to Complex Humanitarian Emergencies from Practice to Policy," Center for Naval Analysis Conference, 26 October 1995, http://www. cna.org/newsevents/conferences/95cf.html.]. *Also see* Erwin A. Schmidl, "The Evolution of Peace Operations from the Nineteenth Century," *Peace Operations Between War and Peace*, Schmidl, ed. (London: Frank Cass, 2000), p. 16.

28. *Washington Post*, August 21, 2000. "Force protection" ordinarily emphasized the dangers emanating from hostile forces; other risks included disease.

29. Michael Ignatieff, "The New American Way of War," *New York Review of Books*, 47 (20 July 2000), p. 42. *Also see* Don M. Snyder, John A. Nagl, and Tony Pfaff, *Army Professionalism, the Military Ethic, and Officership in the 21ˢᵗ Century* (Carlisle, PA; US Army Strategic Studies Institute, 1999), pp. 1-2; Adam Wolfson, "How To Think About Humanitarian War," *Commentary* 110 (July-August 2000), pp. 44-48; Gideon Rose, "The Exit Strategy Delusion," *Foreign Affairs* 77 (January-February 1998), pp. 57-60; William Langewiesche, "Peace Is Hell," *Atlantic Monthly*, 288 (October 2001), p. 76. For the practical effect of this emphasis, illustrated by photographs of a British peacekeeper wearing a beret and an American with his Kevlar helmet, both in Kosovo, *see* Michael R. Gordon, "Looking Like War to Keep the Peace," *New York Times*, 4 February 2001, *Week In Review* section, p. 4.

30. Joyce Howard Price, "Like Osprey Crash, Training Can Be Tragic," *Washington Times*, 29 May 00, p. 1; Robert Novak, "Unknown War

Leaves Victims in Anonymity," *Chicago Sun-Times*, 5 Aug 99, p. 33, cited in Moskos, *The Media and the Military*, endnote 9, p. 53; IFPA, *Summary Report of a Conference On: Operations Other Than War*, p. 6.

31. On the evolution of American policy regarding genocide, *see* Power, "A Problem from Hell," *America and the Age of Genocide*c.

32. Boot, *Savage Wars of Peace*, p. 282.

33. Other names were INTERFET, Stabilize, UNTAET, and USGET.

34. Other names used in regard to the mission in Haiti included Maintain Democracy, Haiti Assistance Group, JTF Raleigh, Phoenix Halibut, Phoenix Shark, Restore Democracy, and United Nations Mission in Haiti (UNMIH).

35. At their peak, American operations in Haiti, involved about 24,000 service members.

36. Holbrooke made these observations on 1 December 2000 in a televised address to a conference on military intervention, held at the George Bush Conference Center, Texas A&M University. For "three different models for international intervention," *see* Erwin A. Schmidl, "Peace Operations: An Assessment," *Europe's New Security Challenges*, Heinz Gärtner, Adrian Hyde-Price, and Erich Reiter, eds. (Boulder, CO: Lynne Rienner, 2001), p. 347.

37. "Verbatim," *Washington Post*, 16 July 2000, p. B2.

Chapter 7

1. Air Mobility Command, which bore the brunt of the workload imposed by presidential travel, did not include presidential missions in its operational chronology. *See* Headquarters Air Mobility Command History Office, *Air Mobility Command: Historical Chronologies* (Scott Air Force Base, IL: n.d.). This document covers the period from June 1992 through September 1997.

2. US General Accounting Office, *Presidential Travel: Costs and Accounting for the President's 1998 Trips to Africa, Chile, and China* (GAO/NSIAD-99-164); John M. Broder, "In the Land of a Billion, a Fitting Presidential Retinue," *New York Times*, June 21, 1998, *Week in Review*, p. 5; Nathan Abse, "Travel Report Riles White House,"

Washington Post, 23 September 1999, p. A27; Ellen Nakashima, "White House Travel Bill: $292 Million," *Washington Post*, 18 August 2000, p. 2; George Lardner, Jr., "Study Names Clinton Most Frequent Flier," *Washington Post*, 16 March 2001, p. A2.

3. Margaret Bone, "Flying Colors," *The Retired Officer Magazine*, 57 (October 2001), p. 58.

4. From 1998 at least into 2000, data on units and aircraft involved in presidential trips, including sorties, units involved, and flying hours, was available on line on the USTRANSCOM, home page, http://tacc.scott.af.mil/ taccapps/custreport/MsnSummaryRpt.asp, as "Mission Summary Reports, Air Mobility Command, February 1999-December 2000" (Downloaded 21 July and 27 December 2000).

5. E-mail message, Robert D. Brunkow to Aaron Horton, 9 April 2001, subject: Information, author's files.

6. Mervin W. Stark, *FORSCOM and the 1996 Summer Olympic Games* (Fort McPherson, GA: US Army Forces Command, 1999), pp. 2-4, 7, 10.

Chapter 8

1. *See* Lawrence J. Korb, "Are US Forces Unprepared and Underfunded? Fact and Fiction," *Naval War College Review*, 55 (Spring 2002), pp. 36-37.

2. US General Accounting Office, *Contingency Operations: Providing Critical Capabilities Poses Challenges* (GAO/NSIAD-00-164), pp. 4-5. *Also see* Bruce D. Callander, "Pressures on the Guard and Reserve," *Air Force Magazine*, November 1998, p. 36.

3. James Morris, *Pax Britannica: the Climax of an Empire* (New York: Harcourt Brace Jovanovich, 1968), p. 405.

4. Quoted in Brian Bond, ed., *Victorian Military Campaigns* (New York: Frederick A. Praeger, 1967), p. 15.

5. James Kitfield, "Standing Apart," *National Journal*, June 13, 1998; the same estimate appears in Don M. Snider, John A. Nagl, and Tony Pfaff, *Army Professionalism, the Military Ethic, and Officership in the 21ˢᵗ Century* (Carlisle, PA; US Army Strategic Studies Institute, 1999), p. 19.

6. Robert Holzer, "US Army, Marines to Gauge Deployment Cost," *Defense News*, 17 July 2000, p. 1.

7. Stephen L. Myers, "Peace Strains the Army," *New York Times, Week in Review*, July 11, 1999. The idea of a "300 percent" increase gained considerable acceptance in just a few months. Snider, Nagl, and Pfaff, *Army Professionalism, the Military Ethic, and Officership in the 21ˢᵗ Century*, p. 19, used it, and General Hugh H. Shelton, the Chairman of the Joint Chiefs of Staff, used it in a speech delivered on March 27, 2001, in Chicago.

8. Greg Parnell, Barry Ezell, Yacov Haimes, James Lambert, Kent Schlussel, and Mark Sulkoski, "Designing a OOTW Knowledge Hierarchy for a OOTW Decision Support System for Military Planners," *Phalanx* 33 (December 2000), pp. 14-19.

9. Paul Mann, "Reframing Objectives Abroad: When To Fight, When Not," *Aviation Week & Space Technology* (31 July 2000), p. 66.

10. *See* Collier, *Instances of Use*, pp. 9-14.

11. William Langewiesche, "Peace Is Hell," *Atlantic Monthly*, 288 (October 2001), p. 52.

12. Gaffney, et al., *US Navy Responses to Situations, 1970-1999*, p. 17.

13. For operations in Vietnam, *see* Appendix E, "A Chronology of the Vietnam War, 1945-1975," *Dictionary of the Vietnam War*, James S. Olson, ed. (Westport, CT: Greenwood Press, 1988), pp. 547-560.

14. Chairman of the Joint Chiefs of Staff, *Report on Military Deployment Rates of the Armed Forces* (March 1999), (S) responded to a Congressional Conference Report (House Report 105-746) on the Appropriations Bill for the Department of Defense, 1998, section 8138. The compilations submitted by the services confirmed that all four used different definitions and methodologies, that all tended to look at overseas exercises as deployments, and that they based deployment rates on "a deployable pool and not a service personnel end strength." Only unclassified sections were used as background material for this study.

15. *Baltimore Sun*, May 24, 1997.

16. The *Baltimore Sun* article cited above overstated the number of soldiers in Germany as 65,000

and those in Korea as 37,000. For official counts of deployed military personnel, of all services, *see* Directorate for Information Operations and Reports, Washington Headquarters Service, Office of the Secretary of Defense, "Military Personnel Historical Reports," (http://web1.whs.osd.mil/mmid/mmidhom.htm). Inflated numbers could be used both to support claims of overwork and to show the pervasiveness of an American presence throughout the world. *See* Harold Perkin, "Stretch marks: the cost of American empire," *Times Literary Supplement* (July 2001), p. 24.

17. Association of the United States Army, "Defense Report," January 2001. *Also see* James Kitfield, "The Peacekeepers," *Government Executive* 33 (March 2001), pp. 44-54, for a supporting view.

18. Directorate for Information Operations and Reports, Washington Headquarters Service, Office of the Secretary of Defense, "Active Duty Military Personnel Strengths by Regional Areas and By Country," on the worldwide web at http://web1.whs.osd.mil/mmid/m65/hst1200.pdf. The Association of the United States Army's display of data to support the claim that the Army is vastly overextended did not end with the 1990s. *See*, especially, Institute of Land Warfare, AUSA, *The Way Ahead* (Arlington, VA: AUSA, July 2000), pp. 5-6. The chart on page 5 shows "Vietnam 1965-75" as one deployment; the similar chart on the following page shows eight separate deployments to Southwest Asia and seven to the Balkans. East Timor, which was the duty station of some of the nine military personnel in Indonesia, is cited as one of multiple obligations.

19. Norman Polmar, Lecture, "The Aircraft Carrier: Anachronism or Force for the Future?" Smithsonian Air and Space Museum, 12 August 1998.

20. Stephen J. Guerra, *Responses to Harm's-Way and Humanitarian Situations by Naval Forces, 1990-1996*, CRM 97-100 (Alexandria, VA: Center for Naval Analyses, 1997), pp. 27-29.

21. US Pacific Command, Command History Division, *Commander in Chief US Pacific Command History, 1990*, vol. 1 (Camp H. M. Smith, Hawaii, 1991), pp. 173-77, 424.

22. Bradley Graham, "US Military Feels Strain of Buildup," *Washington Post*, 5 February 1998, p. 6.

23. US General Accounting Office, *Assets DOD Contributes to Reducing the Illegal Drug Supply Have Declined* (Report No. GAO/NSIAD 00-9, December 1999), p. 22.

24. US General Accounting Office, *Assets DOD Contributes to Reducing the Illegal Drug Supply Have Declined*, p. 7.

25. Brooks and Roller, *Historical Analysis of US Military Responses: 1975-1995*, p. 34.

26. All of these types of aircraft were listed as among "Low Density-High Demand (LDHD) Assets: Unique mission capabilities for crisis responses/contingencies," J-3 Joint Operations Division briefing slide, undated but before 3 June 1999.

27. OPSMSTR9, lines 4686-4791.

28. COL Fred Stein, USA (Ret.), interview with author, 18 December 1997.

29. Mervin W. Stark, *US Army Forces Command Annual Command History, 1 October 1994-31 December 1995* (Fort McPherson, GA: Military History Office, US Army Forces Command, [1998]), chapter 4, p. 11.

30. Stark, *US Army Forces Command Annual Command History, 1 October 1994-31 December 1995*, chapter 4, pp. 6-8.

31. Thomas E. Ricks, "US Military Police Embrace Kosovo Role," *Washington Post*, 25 March 2001, DL Strpce, Yugoslavia.

32. Gwynn, *Imperial Policing*, p. 30.

33. Richard Hart Sinnreich, "Where Are the MPs When We Need Them?" *Lawton* (Oklahoma) *Constitution*, 11 June 2000, p. 4. For a brief look at some of the organizational options for carrying out gendarmerie missions, *see* John S. Brown, "Combat Cops? The Army as Constabulary: Some Lessons From Our Past," *Armed Forces Journal International*, (September 2000), pp. 66-70.

34. David Wood, "Need For MPs Spurs Debate," *Army Times*, 27 March 2000, p. 16.

35. Christine Neuberger, "POW Simulation Exercise Held," *Richmond Times-Dispatch*, 23 June 1998.

36. Walter S. Poole, "The Effort to Save Somalia, August 1992-March 1994," Joint History Office:

draft manuscript, October 2000, (S) pp. 53, 55, 58; Erwin A. Schmidl, "Police in Peace Operations," *Informationen zur Sicherheitspolitik*, Nummer 10 (September 1998), p. 3.

37. Barbara Crossette, "The UN's Unhappy Lot: Perilous Police Duties Multiplying," *New York Times*, 22 February 2000.

38. C. Mark Brinkley, "Warrior Cops: How Kosovo Is Changing Who Deploys—And How You Train," *Marine Corps Times*, 28 February 2000, p. 12.

39. C. Mark Brinkley, "MP Restructuring Step Away From Reality," *Marine Corps Times*, 28 February 2000, p. 14; Brooks and Roller, *Historical Analysis of US Miltary Responses: 1975-1995*, p. 36.

40. Porch, "Introduction," *Small Wars, their Principles & Practice*, by Charles E. Callwell, 3rd (1906) ed. (Lincoln, NE: University of Nebraska Press, 1996), p. xvii.

41. US General Accounting Office, *Contingency Operations: Providing Critical Capabilities Poses Challenges* (GAO/NIAD-00-164), p. 5.

42. Robert Burns, "Shortage of Airborne Jammers Strains Military," *European Stars and Stripes*, 3 October 1999, p. 7; Adam J. Hebert, "Marine Corps Not A Good Place For Air Force To Find Optempo Relief," *Inside the Air Force*, 10 September 1999, p. 3; GAO Report on Contingency Operations July 2000, p. 5.

43. Robert Burns, AP, "Shortage of Airborne Jammers Strains Military," *European Stars and Stripes*, 3 October 1999, p. 7; GAO Report on Contingency Operations Jul 2000, pp. 5-6, 25. Other shortages also seemed to be in highly technical areas. *See* J-3 JOB briefing slide, "Low Density-High Demand (LDHD) Assets: Unique mission capabilities for crisis response/contingencies," undated but before 3 June 1999.

44. US General Accounting Office, *Contingency Operations: Providing Critical Capabilities Poses Challenges*, p. 25.

45. OPSMSTR9, lines 4686-4791; *San Antonio Express-News*, 10 August 1998.

46. Stark, *US Army Forces Command Annual Command History, 1 October 1994-31 December 1995*, chapter 4.

47. OPSMSTR9, lines 4686-4791; Daniel L. Haulman, *The United States Air Force and Humanitarian Airlift Operations 1947-1994* (Washington, DC: Air Force History and Museums Program, 1998), pp. 114-115.

48. Cohen, *Report of the Quadrennial Defense Review*, p. 31. One critic called this approach "a strategy that basically rationalizes much of the existing structure, training and weapon programs of the big, muscular force intended to fight in Europe and to deter a nuclear exchange with the Soviet Union. It also is a strategy that was outdated before it was ever committed to paper. The missions of the American military have changed dramatically since the end of the Cold War. Peacekeeping and humanitarian missions have become the norm. Rather than mobilizing a massive mixed force to a war zone, American military planners find themselves scrambling smaller units to a greater number of hot spots." Bob Kemper, "The US Military Stands Ready—For the Wrong Challenges," *Chicago Tribune*, September 3, 2000.

49. Billy T. Brooks and Kevin Roller, *Historical Analysis of US Military Responses: 1975-1995* (McLean, VA: Science Applications International Corporation, 1996), pp. 10, 37; A. Martin Lidy, M. Michele Cecil, James Kunder, and Samuel H. Packer. *Effectiveness of DOD Humanitarian Relief Efforts in Responses to Hurricanes Georges and Mitch* (IDA Paper P-3560, March 2001), p. ES-5.

50. Frank Wolfe, "Zinni: Strategic Mobility CENTCOM's Greatest Need," *Defense Daily*, 2 March 2000, p. 3.

51. Bradley Graham, "Military Buildup Strains Other Security Commitments," *Washington Post*, 24 Feb 98, p. 17; Brooks and Roller, p. iv; Adam J. Hebert, "Air Force Mission Capable Rates Recover Quickly After Allied Force," *Inside the Air Force*, 8 Oct 99, p. 1; Bruce Rolfsen, "The Busiest Wing," *Air Force Times*, 13 December 1999; Elaine M. Grossman, "Air Force Says Post-Kosovo Recovery Is On Track, But Lacks Data," *Inside the Pentagon*, 30 September 1999; Myers, "Peace Strains the Army," *New York Times*, Sun, 11 Jul 99.

52. The Army units included 6 mobile public affairs detachments of 13 to 18 people each; 2 combat camera units; 2 public affairs teams of 5 each; 1 press camp headquarters detachment of 28; and 1 broadcast detachment with 27 people. The Air Force contributed a 19-person broadcast detachment and a combat camera unit of 39. OPSMSTR9, lines 4686-4791.

53. Moskos, *The Media and the Military in Peace and Humanitarian Operations*, pp. 13, 25; OPSMSTR9, line 4756; Robert D. Kaplan, *Warrior Politics: Why Leadership Demands a Pagan Ethos* (New York: Random House, 2002), pp. 128-129.

54. Telex (U), CINCUSACOM, for CJCS, 302330Z September 1994; Memo, Kenneth H. Bacon, ASD/PA, to CJCS, ca. 24 September 1994, subject: Haiti Updates/Info; Colonel Barry Willey, USA, Ret, telephone conversation with Ronald H. Cole, 3 May 2001. *See* Warren P. Strobel, *Late-Breaking Foreign Policy: the News Media's Influence on Peace Operations* (Washington, DC: United States Institute of Peace Press, 1997), pp. 2, 92-95.

55. Institute for Foreign Policy Analysis, *Summary Report of a Conference On: Operations Other Than War* (Washington: IFPA, 1995), p. v.

56. DSBTF, *Report on DOD Warfighting Transformation*, p. iv, 11-15.

57. "Air Force to Shed Cold War Structure and Reorganize Units," *New York Times*, August 5, 1998, p. A 16, AP, DL Washington, 4 August 1998; "Seeking Stability for USAF's Warriors: An AFJI Interview with General Michael E. Ryan, Chief of Staff, US Air Force," *Armed Forces Journal International*, November 1998, p. 28; Elaine M. Grossman, "Air Force Leaders Embrace Engagement as Force-Sizing Construct," *Inside the Pentagon*, 4 May 2000, p. 1. Glenn W. Goodman, Jr., "Low Density/High Demand: USAF's Limited Numbers of ISR Aircraft Remain Overstretched," *Armed Forces Journal International* (October 2001), pp. 20-21.

58. Frederick L. Borch, *Judge Advocates in Combat: Army Lawyers in Military Operations from Vietnam to Haiti* (Washington, DC: Office of the Judge Advocate General and Center of Military History, US Army, 2001), pp. x, 81-82, 96, 284, 309, 325.

59. On the mobilization of Army reserves for Operations Desert Shield and Desert Storm *see* Frank N. Schubert and Theresa Kraus, eds., *The Whirlwind War: The United States Army in Operations DESERT SHIELD and DESERT STORM* (Washington, DC: United States Army Center of Military History, 1995), pp. 82-92.

60. Mike O'Connor, "Slimmer Army Relies on Reserves for Duty in Bosnia," *New York Times*, 25 May 1998; Robert Holzer, "US Army, Marines To Gauge Deployment Cost," *Defense News*, 17 July 2000, p. 1; US General Accounting Office. *Contingency Operations: Providing Critical Capabilities Poses Challenges* (GAO/NSIAD-00-164, 2000), p. 5; Haulman, *The United States Air Force and Humanitarian Airlift Operations*, passim.

61. On the "Total Force" concept, *see* Jeffrey A. Jacobs, *The Future of the Citizen-Soldier Force: Issues and Answers* (Lexington: The University Press of Kentucky, 1994); Stephen M. Duncan, *Citizen Warriors: America's National Guard and Reserve Forces & the Politics of National Security* (Novato: CA: Presidio Press, 1997).

62. Army News Service, Press Release, "49th Armored Division deploys to Bosnia," 15 February 2000; 29th Division, Press Release, "29th Division part of Army's unit rotation plan for Bosnia," 26 October 1999; *New York Times*, 25 May 1998; Schubert and Kraus, eds., *Whirlwind War*, pp. 57-58; Jacobs, *The Future of the Citizen-Soldier Force*, p. 94.

63. Carroll H. Dunn, *Base Development in South Vietnam 1965-1970* (Washington, DC: Department of the Army, 1972), p. 25.

64. *See* Janet A. McDonnell, *The Logistics Civil Augmentation Program (LOGCAP): Supporting the Troops in Operation Restore Hope* (Alexandria, VA: Headquarters, US Army Corps of Engineers, 1994); Donald T. Wynn, "Managing the Logistics-Support Contract in the Balkans Theater," *Engineer* 30 (July 2000), pp. 36-40. Regarding contractors as an alternative for functions such as medical treatment, supply, housing construction, and transportation, see the following US General Accounting Office reports: *Contingency Operations: Army Should Do More to Control Contract Cost in the Balkans* (GAO/NSIAD-00-225, Sep 29, 2000); *Contingency Operations: Opportunities to Improve the Logistics Civil Augmentation Program* (GAO/NSIAD-97-63, Feb. 11, 1997).

65. US General Accounting Office, *Contingency Operations: Providing Critical Capabilities Poses Challenges* (GAO/NIAD-00-164), pp. 7-8.

66. Cohen, *Report of the Quadrennial Defense Review*, p. 36.

67. Cohen, *Major Smaller Scale Contingencies*, pp. 26-27.

68. US General Accounting Office. *Contingency Operations: Providing Critical Capabilities Poses Challenges* (GAO/NSIAD-00-164, 2000), p. 25.

69. Admiral James O. Ellis, briefing, "A View from the Top," ca. September 1999.

70. Frank N. Schubert, *Building Air Bases in the Negev: the US Army Corps of Engineers in Israel, 1979-1982* (Washington, DC: Office of History, Corps of Engineers and Center of Military History, US Army, 1992), p. 33.

71. Brooks and Roller, *Historical Analysis of US Military Responses: 1975-1995*, p. vi.

72. *New York Times*, 1 September 1998; Brooks and Roller, *Historical Analysis of US Military Responses*, pp. 28, 32.

73. Max Boot, "Will Bush Bury 'Bodybag Syndrome'?" *Wall Street Journal*, 11 Sep 2000, p. 44.

74. Elizabeth Becker, "The Dangers of Doing Good Deeds," *New York Times*, Sunday, 6 January 2002, *Week In Review*, p. 4.

Chapter 9

1. The quotation is from Kenneth Anderson, "Language, law, and terror," (London) *Times Literary Supplement*, 21 September 2001. For two insightful looks at the nature of the terrorist enemy and the response, see that essay and Anderson, "Expanded Horizons: Memory, Memorials and Manhattan's Living Skyline," Ibid., 6 September 2002.

2. Air Mobility Command History Office, *Air Mobility Command: Historical Chronologies. June 1992-September 1997*, revision thru Mar 1998, received from AMCHO History Office, Jul 2000.

3. Chivers, "Long Before War, Green Berets Built Military Ties to Uzbekistan," *New York Times*, 25 Oct 01, DL Tashkent, 24 Oct 01, p. 1. On the Joint Contact Team program, *see* Robert T. Cossaboom, *The Joint Contact Team Program: Contacts with Former Soviet Republics and Warsaw Pact Nations 1992-1994* (Washington, DC: Joint History Office, 1997).

4. Joseph Lelyveld, "In Guantanamo," *New York Review of Books* 44 (November 17, 2002), p. 64.

5. Dana Priest, "US Military Trains Foreign Troops," *Washington Post,* 12 July 1998; Michael P. Noonan and John Hillen, "The Promise of Decisive Action," *Orbis,* 46 (Spring 2002), p. 239.

6. US General Accounting Office, *Drug Control: DOD Allocates Fewer Assets to Drug Control Efforts,* GAO/NSIAD 00-77; Dennis Jett, "Remember the Drug War?" *Washington Post*, Sunday, 13 January 2002, Outlook, p. B4.

7. Boot, *Savage Wars of Peace*, p. xiv.

Bibliography

Abbott, Catherine. "Utilization of New Zealand Defence Force Capabilities on International Stability and Military Operations 1946-1998." Unpublished mss.

Air Mobility Command History Office. Air Mobility Command: Historical Chronologies. June 1992-September 1997, revised through June 1998.

Alvarez, José E. *The Betrothed of Death: The Spanish Foreign Legion during the Rif Rebellion, 1920-1927*. Westport, CT: Greenwood Press, 2001.

Anderson, Kenneth. "Language, Law and Terror," *TLS*, No. 5138 (21 September 2001), pp. 13-15.

Australian Maritime Doctrine: RAN Doctrine 1, 2000. Canberra: Defence Publishing Service, 2000.

Axtman, Kris. "Work-Family Issues Rank, Even in the Army," *Christian Science Monitor*, 8 March 2000, p. 2

Birtle, Andrew J. *US Army Counterinsurgency and Contingency Operations Doctrine, 1860-1941*. Washington, DC: US Army Center of Military History, 1998.

Blechman, Barry M. and Stephen S. Kaplan. *Force Without War: US Armed Forces as a Political Instrument*. Washington, DC: Brookings Institution, 1978.

Bond, Brian, ed. *Victorian Military Campaigns*. New York: Frederick A. Praeger, 1967.

Bone, Margaret. "Flying Colors," *The Retired Officer Magazine*, 57 (October 2001), pp. 56-62.

Boot, Max. *The Savage Wars of Peace: Small Wars and the Rise of American Power*. New York: Basic Books, 2002.

Boot, Max. "Will Bush Bury 'Bodybag Syndrome'?" *Wall Street Journal*, 11 Sep 2000, p. 44.

Borch, Frederic L. *Judge Advocates in Combat: Army Lawyers in Military Operations from Vietnam to Haiti.* Washington, DC: Office of the Judge Advocate General and Center of Military History, US Army, 2001.

Brinkley, C. Mark. "Warrior Cops: How Kosovo Is Changing Who Deploys— And How You Train," *Marine Corps Times*, 28 February 2000, p. 12.

Brinkley, C. Mark. "MP Restructuring A Step Away From Reality," *Marine Corps Times*, 28 February 2000, p. 14.

Brooks, Billy T. and Kevin Roller. Historical Analysis of US Military Responses: 1975-1995. McLean, VA: Science Applications International Corporation, 1996.

Brown, John S. "Combat Cops? The Army as Constabulary: Lessons From Our Past," *Armed Forces Journal International* (September 2000), pp. 66-70.

Browne, Marjorie Ann. "United Nations Peacekeeping: Issues for Congress," CRS Report, Order Code IB90103, 2 April 1996.

Browne, Marjorie Ann. "United Nations Peacekeeping Operations, 1988-1993: Background Information," CRS Report No. 94-193 F, 28 February 1994.

Bruner, Edward F. and Nina M. Serafino. *Peacekeeping: Military Command and Control Issues,* CRS Report for Congress, 1 Nov 2001.

Buchanan, Wayne, Captain, USCG, J-33, JS. Major Smaller Scale Contingency Operations from 1990-Present. Excel spreadsheet. July 2000.

Burns, Robert (AP), "Shortage of Airborne Jammers Strains Military," *European Stars and Stripes*, DL Whidbey Island Naval Air Station, WA, 3 October 1999, p. 7

Callander, Bruce D. "Pressures on the Guard and Reserve," *Air Force Magazine*, Nov 1998, p. 36.

Callwell, Charles E. *Small Wars, their Principles & Practice.* 3rd ed. (1906), Lincoln, NE: University of Nebraska Press, 1996. Introduction to Bison Book edition by Douglas Porch.

(S) Chairman of the Joint Chiefs of Staff. *Report on Military Deployment Rates of the Armed Forces.* March 1999.

Coffman, Edward M. "The Duality of the American Military Tradition," *Journal of Military History* 64 (October 2000), pp. 967-980.

Cohen, Eliot A. "Defending America in the Twenty-first Century," *Foreign Affairs* 79 (November-December 2000), pp. 40-56.

Cohen, William S. (Secretary of Defense) *Report of the Quadrennial Defense Review.* May 1997.

_____. *Report to Congress on US Military Involvement in Major Smaller-Scale Contingencies Since the Persian Gulf War.* Washington: OSD, March 1999. Cited as Cohen, *Major Smaller-Scale Contingencies.*

The Commission on America's National Interests. *America's National Interests.* July 2000. http://www.nixoncenter.org/publications/monographs/nationalinterests. pdf.

Cook, Frank J., III, Jeffrey A. McChesney, Gary R. Stephens, Gregory G. Wilmoth, and William M. Wilson. *The Defense Department's Role in Humanitarian and Disaster Relief.* John F. Kennedy School of Government National Security Program Policy Analysis Paper 93-02. Cambridge: Harvard University, 1993.

Correll, John T. "Northern Watch: a wing-sized task force flies out of Incirlik into the teeth of Iraqi SAMs and AAA," *Air Force Magazine* (February 2000).

Crossette, Barbara. "The UN's Unhappy Lot: Perilous Police Duties Multiplying," *NY Times,* Tue, 22 Feb 2000, p. A3, DL United Nations, 21 Feb 2000.

Daggett, Stephen. "Incremental Costs of DOD Contingency Operations, FY1991-1999," 31 December 99.

Defense Science Board Task Force. *Report on DOD Warfighting Transformation.* Washington: Office of the Undersecretary of Defense for Acquisition and Technology, [September] 1999.

Deutsch, Karl W. and William J. Foltz, eds. *Nation-Building.* New York: Atherton Press, 1966.

DFI International. "USAF Presence Database." 24 pp.

Dixon, Anne M. and Maureen A. Wigge, eds. *Military Support to Complex Humanitarian Emergencies: From Practice to Policy.* CAN 1995 Annual Conference Proceedings. Alexandria, VA: CNA, n.d.

Doyle, Frances M., Karen J. Lewis, and Leslie A. Williams. "Named Military Operations from January 1989 to December 1993." Fort Monroe: TRADOC Technical Library, April 1994.

Dunn, Timothy J. *The Militarization of the US-Mexican Border, 1872-1992: Low-Intensity Conflict Comes Home.* Austin: The Center for Mexican American Studies, The University of Texas at Austin, 1996.

Ensign, Eric S. *Intelligence in the Rum War at Sea, 1920-1933.* Washington, DC: Joint Military Intelligence College, 2001.

Epley, William W., comp. *Roles and Missions of the United States Army: Basic Documents with Annotations and Bibliography.* Washington, DC: US Army Center of Military History, 1991.

Federation of American Scientists. United States Military Operations. 31 March 1998. (http://www.fas.org/man/dod-101/ops/.

Ferguson, Nial. "War Names," *New York Times Magazine* (15 December 2002), pp. 39-40, 42.

Ferrante, Ann M. "Chronology of the United States Marine Corps," 1989-2000.

Fisher, Ian. "Can International Relief Do More Good Than Harm?" *New York Times Magazine*, 11 February 2001).

_____. "Congo's War Triumphs Over Peace Accord," *NY Times*, Mon, September 18, 2000, pp. 1, 8, DL Dongo, Congo, 13 Sep 2000.

Fleitz, Frederick H., Jr. *Peacekeeping Fiascoes of the 1990s: Causes, Solutions, and US Interests.* Westport, CT: Praeger, 1902.

Fox, John G. "Approaching Humanitarian Intervention Strategically: The Case of Somalia," *Essays 2000* (Washington, DC: NDU Press, 2000).

Furman, H. W. C. "Restrictions Upon Use of the Army Imposed by the Posse Comitatus Act," *Military Law Review* 7 (January 1960), pp. 85-129.

Gaffney, Henry H., Jr., Eugene Cobble, Dmitry Gorenburg, Adam Moody, Richard Weitz, and Daniel Whiteneck. *US Navy Responses to Situations, 1970-1999.* Alexandria, VA: Center for Naval Analyses, 2000.

Gates, John M. "Indians and Insurrectos: the US Army's Experience with Insurgency," chapter two, of Gates, *The US Army and Irregular Warfare.* Published on line at http://www.wooster. edu/history/jgates/book-ch2.html (as of Dec 2000).

Gilpin, Robert. *Global Political Economy: Understanding the International Economic Order.* Princeton, NJ: Princeton University Press, 2001.

Gongora, Thierry and Harald von Riekhoff, eds. *Toward a Revolution in Military Affairs: Defense and Security at the Dawn of the Twenty-First Century.* Westport, CT: Greenwood Press, 2000.

Goodman, Glenn W., Jr. "Low Density/High Demand: USAF's Limited Numbers of ISR Aircraft Remain Overstretched," *Armed Forces Journal International* (October 2001), pp. 20-21.

Gourevitch, Philip. "Forsaken: How a seven-nation war engulfed Congo," *New Yorker*, September 25, 2000.

Grossman, Elaine M. "Air Force Leaders Embrace Engagement as Force-Sizing Construct," *Inside the Pentagon*, 4 May 2000.

Grossman, Elaine M. "Air Force Says Post-Kosovo Recovery Is On Track, But Lacks Data," *Inside the Pentagon*, 30 September 1999.

Guerra, Stephen J. *Responses to Harm's-Way and Humanitarian Situations by Naval Forces, 1990-1996.* CRM 97-100. Alexandria, VA: Center for Naval Analyses, 1997.

Guthman, William H. *March to Massacre: a History of the First Seven Years of the United States Army 1784-1791.* New York: McGraw-Hill Book Company, 1975.

Gwynn, Charles W. *Imperial Policing.* London: Macmillan and Co., Ltd., 1934, 1939.

Hagan, Kenneth J. *This People's Navy: The Making of American Sea Power.* New York: The Free Press, 1991.

Halberstam, David. *War in a Time of Peace: Bush, Clinton, and the Generals.* New York: Scribner, 2001.

Harden, Blaine. "The US Keeps Looking for a Few Good Men," *New York Times*, Week In Review, Sunday, 27 August 2000, pp. 1, 5.

Haulman, Daniel L. *The United States Air Force and Humanitarian Airlift Operations 1947-1994.* Washington, DC: Air Force History and Museums Program, 1998.

Hebert, Adam J. "Air Force Mission Capable Rates Recover Quickly After Allied Force," *Inside the Air Force,* 8 Oct 99, p. 1.

Hebert, Adam J. "Marine Corps Not A Good Place For Air Force To Find Optempo Relief," *Inside the Air Force,* 10 Sep 99, p. 3.

Henk, Dan. *Uncharted Paths, Uncertain Vision: US Military Involvements in Sub-Saharan Africa in the Wake of the Cold War.* INSS Occasional Paper 18. Colorado Springs: USAF Institute for National Security Studies, 1998.

Hillen, John. *Blue Helmets: The Strategy of UN Military Operations* Washington: Brassey's, 1998.

Historical Services Division, National Guard Bureau. *History of the Air National Guard January 1986-December 1991.* n.d.

Historical Services Division, National Guard Bureau. *History of the Air National Guard January 1992-December 1994.* July 1996.

Historical Services Division, National Guard Bureau. *History of the Air National Guard January 1995-December 1997.* July 1998.

Hofstetter, Melinda. *Building Alliances Amidst Destruction: A Status Report from Hurricane Mitch.* Discussion paper Number Nine. Washington, DC: Joint Military Intelligence College, 2000.

Holzer, Robert. "US Army, Marines To Gauge Deployment Cost," *Defense News,* 17 July 2000, p. 1.

Hottelet, Richard C. "Moving Beyond Makeshift Peacekeeping," *Christian Science Monitor,* 27 Sep 2000, p. 11, DL Wilton, CT.

Ignatieff, Michael. "The New American Way of War," *New York Review of Books,* 47 (20 July 2000), pp. 42-46.

Immigration & Refugee Services of America. *Lessons Learned: Operation Pacific Haven, September 1996-1997.* Summary of Roundtable Discussions Convened in August 1997.

Institute for Foreign Policy Analysis. *Summary Report of a Conference On: Operations Other Than War.* Washington: IFPA, 1995.

Institute of Land Warfare, AUSA. *The Way Ahead.* Arlington, VA: AUSA, July 2000.

InterAction. "Rwanda Crisis Situation Report No. 10 Draft," 20 October 1994.

International Federation of Red Cross and Red Crescent Societies. *World Disasters Report 1996.* New York: Oxford University Press, 1996.

_____. *World Disasters Report 2000: Focus on Public Health.* Peter Walker and Jonathan Walter, eds. Geneva: International Federation of Red Cross and Red Crescent Societies, 2000.

James, C. Neil. "A Brief History of Australian Peacekeeping." Unpublished manuscript, n.d., author's files.

James, Lawrence. *The Savage Wars: British Campaigns in Africa, 1870-1902.* New York: St. Martin's Press, 1985.

Jamieson, Perry D. *Crossing the Deadly Ground: United States Army Tactics, 1865-1899.* Tuscaloosa, AL: University of Alabama Press, 1994.

Jencks, Christopher. "Who Should Get In? Part II," *New York Review of Books,* 48 (December 20, 2001), pp. 94-102.

(C) Joint Interagency Task Force East. Briefing: Counter Drug Operations Index. 1 August 1999. "Confidential Rel UK/NL/FR."

(S) Joint Staff Response Team. Kosovo Crisis Response. Briefing. SECRET. 18 June 1999.

J-3 Newcomer's Training, Powerpoint Slide Presentation, Joint Staff Intranet, as of 15 October 1997.

Kagan, Robert. *Of Paradise and Power: America and Europe in the New World Order.* New York: Alfred A. Knopf, 2003.

Kaplan, Robert D. *Warrior Politics: Why Leadership Demands a Pagan Ethos.* New York: Random House, 2002.

Keller, Bill. "The Fighting Next Time," *New York Times Magazine,* March 10, 2002.

Kennedy, Paul. *The Rise and Fall of the Great Powers.* New York: Random House, 1987.

Kersten, Andrew E. and Kriste Lendenmeyer, eds. *Politics and Progress: American Society and the State since 1865.* Westport, CT: Praeger, 2001.

Kitfield, James. "Peacekeepers' Progress," *National Journal,* 32 (December 2000).

_____. "The Hollow Force Myth," *Government Executive,* 31 (January 1999), pp. 58-59.

_____. "The Peacekeepers," *Government Executive,* 33 (March 2001), pp. 44-54.

Langewiesche, William. "Peace Is Hell," *Atlantic Monthly,* 288 (October 2001), pp. 51-58, 60, 62-67, 70-74, 76, 78-80.

Langley, Lester D. *The Banana Wars: United States Intervention in the Caribbean, 1898-1934.* Wilmington, DE: Scholarly Resources, 2002.

Lawford, James P. *Britain's Army in India, from its Origins to the Conquest of Bengal.* London: George Allen & Unwin, 1978.

Leland, John W. *Operation Provide Hope, February 1992-April 1993.* Scott Air Force Base, IL: Office of History, Air Mobility Command, 1993.

Lelyveld, Joseph. "In Guantanamo," *New York Review of Books* 44 (November 17, 2002).

Lewis, Karen. "Named Military Operations 1993-1996." Fort Monroe: TRADOC Technical Library.

Lidy, A. Martin, David Arthur, James Kunder, and Samuel H. Packer. *Bosnia Air Drop Study.* IDA Paper P-3474, September 1999.

Lidy, A. Martin, M. Michele Cecil, James Kunder, and Samuel H. Packer. *Effectiveness of DOD Humanitarian Relief Efforts in Responses to Hurricanes Georges and Mitch.* IDA Paper P-3560, March 2001.

Linderman, Gerald F. *The Mirror of War: American Society and the Spanish-American War* (Ann Arbor: University of Michigan Press, 1974).

Linenthal, Edward T. *Sacred Ground: Americans and their Battlefields.* Urbana: University of Illinois Press, 1991.

Luttwak, Edward. "A Post-Heroic Military Policy," *Foreign Affairs* 75 (June-August 1996), 33-44.

Maher, John III (MG, USA; Vice J-3). Briefing on Response to Hurricane Mitch, Pentagon, 25 November 1998.

Mandelbaum, Michael. Foreign Policy as Social Work," *Foreign Affairs,* 75 (January-February 1996), pp. 16-32.

Mann, Paul. "Reframing Objectives Abroad: When To Fight, When Not," *Aviation Week & Space Technology* (31 July 2000), p. 66.

Martinez, Ruben. *Crossing Over: A Mexican Family on the Migrant Trail.* New York: Metropolitan Books/Henry Holt & Company, 2002.

Matloff, Maurice, ed. *American Military History.* Washington, DC: US Army Center of Military History, 1989.

Matthews, James K. (TRANSCOM historian). Issue Paper, subject: Precedent and Possible Rationale for and against USCINCTRANs to be SUPPORTED CINC in the Former Soviet Union, 12 April 1996.

_____. *United States Transportation Command History*, Volume II, *1 January 1990-31 December 1990.* Scott AFB, IL: USTRANSCOM Office of History 1992.

_____. *United States Transportation Command, the National Defense Reserve Fleet, and the Ready Reserve Force: A Chronology.* Scott AFB, IL: United States Transportation Command Research Center, 1997.

_____. *United States Transportation Command, the National Defense Reserve Fleet, and the Ready Reserve Force: A Chronology.* Scott AFB, IL: United States Transportation Command Research Center, 1999.

McElroy, MAJ Terry. "DCMC at work in the Balkans," *Dimensions* (Sep-Oct 1999), pp. 22-23.

McNeill, William H. *The Pursuit of Power: Technology, Armed Force, and Society since AD 1000*. Chicago: University of Chicago Press, 1982.

Miller, Benjamin. "The Logic of US Military Interventions in the post-Cold War Era," *Contemporary Security Policy*, 19 (December 1998).

Millett, Allan R., and Peter Maslowski. *For the Common Defense: a Military History of the United States of America*. New York: Macmillan, 1984.

Mockaitis, Thomas R. *British Counterinsurgency, 1919-1960*. NY: St. Martin's Press, 1990.

(S-NF) Monroe, Alexander M. *US Atlantic Command Support of Counterdrug Operations in the Caribbean 1989-1997*. Norfolk, VA: Office of the Command Historian, HQ, USJFC, 2000.

(U) Morgan, COL John W. "Army Regulation (AR) 15-6 Report of Investigation (ROI)," with enclosures, 25 February 2000.

Morris, James. *Pax Britannica: the Climax of an Empire*. New York: Harcourt Brace Jovanovich, 1968.

Moskos, Charles C. *The Media and the Military in Peace and Humanitarian Operations*. Chicago: McCormick Tribune Foundation, 2000. Cantigny Conference Series special report.

Myers, Steven Lee. "Peace Strains the Army," *New York Times*, Sunday, 11 July 1999, Week in Review, p. 4. (DL Washington)

_____. "New Role of Guard Transforming Military," *New York Times*, Mon, 24 Jan 2000, p. A22, DL Austin, 17 Jan 2000.

Nakashima, Ellen. "White House Travel Bill: $292 Million," *Washington Post*, 18 Aug 2000, p. 2.

Neil, LTC James. "A Brief History of Australian Peacekeeping." Unpublished manuscript in Schubert files.

Nelson, Lars-Erik. "Armed to the Teeth," *New York Daily News*, 3 Sep 2000, DL Washington.

Noonan, Michael P. and John Hillen, "The Promise of Decisive Action," *Orbis*, 46 (Spring 2002), pp. 229-246.

Nordland, Rod. "Saddam's Long Shadow," *Newsweek,* 31 July 2000, p. 32.

OCJCS (PA). List of Current and Past US Military Operations (1990-Present). 6 May 1997.

Operation Deliberate Force: the UN and NATO Campaign in Bosnia, 1995. Bailrigg Study 3. Lancaster: Center for Defence and International Security Studies, n.d.

OSD (Comptroller), "DOD Contingency Operations/Humanitarian Assistance Program Incremental Costs, FY 1992-1995," n.d. Cited as "OSD Contingency Costs."

Pacific Stars and Stripes, 1998.

Parnell, Greg, Barry Ezell, Yacov Haimes, James Lambert, Kent Schlussel, and Mark Sulkoski. "Designing a OOTW Knowledge Hierarchy for a OOTW Decision Support System for Military Planners," Phalanx, 33 (December 2000), pp. 14-19.

Passage, David. "Latin America: The Next Quarter-Century Challenges and Opportunities," *Roles and Missions of SOF in the Aftermath of the Cold War,* edited by Richard H. Shultz, Jr., Robert L. Pfaltzgraff, Jr., and W. Bradley Stock (N.P.: N.p.).

Philpott, Tom. "The US Navy in 2000: An Unprecedented Pace of Operations," *Sea Power* 44, no. 1 (January 2000).

Pitts, John. "Engaging Adversity: US Southern Command and the International Effort to Aid the Countries Devastated by Hurricanes Georges and Mitch." Unpublished manuscript, c. 2000.

_____. Letter (e-mail) to Frank N. Schubert, 5 January 2001, subject: USSOUTHCOM CD Ops.

_____. *Migrant Resettlement Operations.* Supplement Nr. 2 to US Southern Command History for 1 January 1994-31 December 1995. Miami, FL: Office of the Command Historian, 1998.

(S) _____. *United States Southern Command, Command History: Tenure of General Barry R. McCaffrey, February 1994-February 1996.* Miami, FL: Office of the Command Historian, 1998.

(S) Poole, Walter S. "The Effort to Save Somalia, August 1992-March 1994." Joint History Office: Draft manuscript, October 2000. (S)

Power, Samantha. *"A Problem from Hell:" America and the Age of Genocide.* New York: Basic Books, 2002.

Raines, Edgar F., Jr. Information Paper, subject: The Army's Role in Disaster Relief—A Historical Perspective, 9 August 1994.

Rand Corporation (Bruce Pirnie). List of Operations, 1990-1996. Attachment to letter, Pirnie to David A. Armstrong, 11 Oct 1996.

Rand Corporation. Recent Operations Data Base.

Reader, Ned, to Robby Robinson, memorandum. subject: Personnel Statistics for Selected US Military Operations, [8 April 1997].

Record, Jeffrey. "Collapsed Countries, Casualty Dread, and the New American Way of War," *Parameters* 32 (Summer 2002), 4-23.

Resource Guide, Unified Task Force Somalia, December 1992–May 1993. Washington, DC: US Army Center of Military History, 1994.

Richter, Paul. "Kosovo Report Supports Calls for Separate Army Peacekeeping Force," *Los Angeles Times*, 22 September 2000, DL Washington.

Ricks, Thomas E. "Persian Gulf, US Danger Zone," *Washington Post*, Sunday, 15 October 2000, pp. A1, A23.

_____. "US Military Police Embrace Kosovo Role," *Washington Post*, Sunday, 25 March 20001, DL Strpce, Yugoslavia, p. 21.

(U) Rippe, Major General Stephen T., USA. Memorandum for the Commander, Joint Task Force–Computer Network Defense, SUBJECT: JTF-CND Concept of Operations, 30 December 1998.

Rolfsen, Bruce. "The Busiest Wing," *Air Force Times*. 13 December 1999.

Rose, Gideon. "The Exit Strategy Delusion," *Foreign Affairs* 77 (January-February 1998).

Sadowski, Yahya. *The Myth of Global Chaos.* Washington, DC: Brookings Institution Press, 1998.

Schaffer, Ronald. "The 1940 Small Wars Manual and the 'Lessons of History,'" introduction to *Small Wars Manual, United States Marine Corps, 1940.* Manhattan, KS: Sunflower University Press, 1989.

Shelton, Henry H. "Remarks," Mid-America Committee Leadership Luncheon, The Mid-America Club, Chicago, IL, Monday, 26 March 2001.

Schmidl, Erwin A., ed. *Peace Operations Between War and Peace.* London: Frank Cass, 2000.

_____. "Police in Peace Operations," *Informationen zur Sicherheitspolitik,* Nummer 10 (September 1998).

Schneider, Greg and Tom Ricks. "Cheney's Firm Profited From 'Overused' Army, *Washington Post,* 9 September 2000, p. 6.

Schubert, Frank N., ed. *The Nation Builders: A Sesquicentennial History of the Corps of Topographical Engineers, 1838-1863.* Fort Belvoir, VA: Office of History, US Army Corps of Engineers, 1988.

_____. *Vanguard of Expansion: Army Engineers in the Trans-Mississippi West 1819-1879.* Washington, DC: Historical Division, Office of the Chief of Engineers, 1980.

Shultz, Richard H., Jr. *In the Aftermath of War: US Support for Reconstruction and Nation-Building in Panama Following Just Cause.* Maxwell Air Force Base, AL: Air University Press, 1993.

Sicherman, Harvey. "Finding a Foreign Policy," *Orbis* 46 (Spring 2002), pp. 215-227.

Sinai, Joshua. Draft List of Operations, 1975-1995.

Snider, Don M., John A. Nagl, and Tony Pfaff. *Army Professionalism, the Military Ethic, and Officership in the 21st Century.* Carlisle, PA; US Army Strategic Studies Institute, 1999.

Stark, Mervin W. *US Army Forces Command Annual Command History, 1 October 1994-31 December 1995.* Fort McPherson, GA: Military History Office, US Army Forces Command, [1998].

_____. *US Army Forces Command Annual Command History, 1 January 1996-31 December 1996.* Fort McPherson, GA: Military History Office, US Army Forces Command, [1998].

_____. *US Army Forces Command Annual Command History, 1 January 1997-31 December 1997.* Fort McPherson, GA: Military History Office, US Army Forces Command, [1998].

_____. *US Army Forces Command Annual Command History, 1 January 1998-31 December 1998.* Fort McPherson, GA: Military History Office, US Army Forces Command, [1998].

Stevenson, Jonathan. *Losing Mogadishu: Testing US Policy in Somalia.* Annapolis: Naval Institute Press, 1995.

Stewart, George, Scott M. Fabbri, and Adam B. Siegel. *JTF Operations since 1983.* Alexandria, VA: Center for Naval Analyses, 1994.

Suro, Roberto. "Smuggling Patrols Face Violence at Sea," *Washington Post*, Thursday, 27 January 2000, pp. A1, A11.

_____. "Up In Arms," *Washington Post*, Monday, 21 August 2000, p. 19.

Swartz, Peter M. and E. D. McGrady. *A Deep Legacy: Smaller-Scale Contingencies and the Forces Than Shape the Navy.* Alexandria, VA: Center for Naval Analyses, 1998.

Sweetman, Jack. *American Naval History: An Illustrated Chronology of the US Navy and Marine Corps, 1775-Present.* Annapolis: Naval Institute Press, 1991.

Tate, Michael L. *The Frontier Army in the Settlement of the West.* Norman: University of Oklahoma Press, 1999.

Troshinsky, Lisa. "Study Changes 'Two MTW' Standard, But Lacks Measuring Tools," *Navy News & Undersea Technology*, 2 October 2000, p. 1.

Turley, Gerald H. "Prepare for the Most Likely Commitments," *Proceedings of the US Naval Institute* (April 2001), pp. 88-89.

US Congress. House of Representatives. *Communication from the President of the United States Transmitting a Report on Progress Made Toward Achieving Benchmarks for a Sustainable Peace Process.* 106th Congress, 2nd Session, House Document 106-231. Washington, DC: Government Printing Office, 2000.

US Agency for International Development, Bureau for Humanitarian Response, Office of US Foreign Disaster Assistance (OFDA). "Rwanda— Civil Strife/Displaced Persons Situation Report #1 Fiscal Year (FY) 1995." 17 October 1994.

US Air Forces Europe/History Office (Dan Harrington). Recent USAFE Contingencies. 17 Mar 1997.

_____. Recent USAFE Contingencies. 19 Jan 1999.

_____. Recent USAFE Contingencies. 1 Nov 2001.

US Air Mobility Command homepage. (Http://www.amc.af.mil) 21 Jul 1999.

US Army Corps of Engineers (Military Programs Directorate). "LOGCAP: A Chronological Program & Contract Overview." n.d.

(S) US Army Europe/7th Army. *Command History, 1 January 1992-31 December 1992.* December 1993.

(S) USAREUR/7th Army. *Command History, 1 January 1993-31 December 1995.* December 1999.

US Army Reserve Command. "Joint Task Force ?? New Horizons 99-02," briefing slides [Feb 99].

US Atlantic Command homepage (SIPRNET). Command Duty Officer On Line, October 1998- .

(S) US Central Command. "Operation ENDURING FREEDOM: Chronology, 11 Sep 01-5 Feb 02."

US European Command, Logistics and Security Assistance Directorate (ECJ4). "Kosovo Campaign Logistics." Briefing slides, 15 Sep 1999.

_____. Historian. "USEUCOM Operations 1989-Present." [1999] In JHO files.

_____. Historian. "USEUCOM Operations Since 1989." 24 September 1902. In JHO files.

US General Accounting Office. *Contingency Operations: Army Should Do More to Control Contract Cost in the Balkans.* GAO/NSIAD-00-225.

US General Accounting Office. *Contingency Operations: DOD's Reported Costs Contain Significant Inaccuracies.* GAO/NSIAD-96-115.

US General Accounting Office. *Contingency Operations: Opportunities to Improve the Logistics Civil Augmentation Program.* GAO/NSAID-97-63.

US General Accounting Office. *Contingency Operations: Providing Critical Capabilities Poses Challenges.* GAO/NSIAD-00-164.

US General Accounting Office. *Contingency Operations: Update on DOD's Fiscal Year 1995 Cost and Funding.* GAO/NSIAD-96-184BR.

US General Accounting Office. *Defense Budget: Fiscal Year 2000 Contingency Operations Costs and Funding.* GAO/NSAID-00-168.

US General Accounting Office. *Drug Control: Assets DOD Contributes to Reducing the Illegal Drug Supply Have Declined.* GAO/NSIAD 00-9.

US General Accounting Office. *Drug Control: DOD Allocates Fewer Assets to Drug Control Efforts.* GAO/NSIAD 00-77.

_____. *Military Personnel: Full Extent of Support to Civil Authorities Unknown but Unlikely to Adversely Impact Retention.* GAO-01-9.

US General Accounting Office. *Presidential Travel: Costs and Accounting for the President's 1998 Trips to Africa, Chile, and China.* GAO/NSIAD-99-164.

USN homepage (DEFENSELINK). "Forces in the 5th Fleet Area of Operations." As of 18 Dec 98, order of battle for Operation DESERT FOX.

USN homepage (SIPRNET). Crisis Response Summary, 1962-1998.

US PACOM. Command History Division. *Commander in Chief US Pacific Command History, 1990.* 2 vols. Camp H. M. Smith, Hawaii, 1991.

US PACOM. Command History Division. *Commander in Chief US Pacific Command History, 1991.* 2 vols. Camp H. M. Smith, Hawaii, 1992.

US SOCOM. *History.* 3rd ed. 1999.

US SOUTHCOM. Command Historian (John A. Pitts). Background paper. Subject: Milestones in the Evolution of SouthCom's Counterdrug Mission, 21 May 1996.

US SOUTHCOM. Command Historian (John A. Pitts). "Historical Files and Archival Media of US Southern Comand: Accessions as of 30 June 1994." Circular No. 5, Counterdrugs.

(S) US SOUTHCOM. Command Historian (John A. Pitts). *United States Southern Command Command History January 1990-December 1991*. 3 vols. Quarry Heights, Panama: Office of the Command Historian, 1994.

(S) US SOUTHCOM. Command Historian (John A. Pitts). *United States Southern Command Command History January 1992-December 1993*. 2 vols. Quarry Heights, Panama: Office of the Command Historian, 1994.

US TRANSCOM. Home page: http://tacc.scott.af.mil/taccapps/ custreport/ MsnSummaryRpt.asp. Mission summary reports, Air Mobility Command, February 1999-July 2000. Downloaded 21 Jul 2000.

Urquhart, Bryan. "How Not to Deal with Bullies," *New York Review of Books* 47 (21 September 2000).

Utley, Robert M. "The Contribution of the Frontier to the American Military Tradition." In *The Harmon Memorial Lectures in Military History, 1959-1987*, edited by Harry R. Borowski. Washington, DC: Office of Air Force History, 1988.

Van Sweringen, Bryan T. "Mission and Resources for 'A Theater in Conflict:' The US European Command (USEUCOM) After the Cold War," unpublished paper, 1995, in author's files.

_____. Outline for Oral History Interview with General George A. Joulwan. July 1997.

Vaughn, Chris. "Increasing Deployments Weighing Heavily on Reserves, Guard," *Fort Worth Star-Telegram*, 6 Feb 2000, p. 1.

Vision … Presence … Power …: A Program Guide to the US Navy. 1999 Edition. Washington, DC: Department of the Navy, 1999.

Vogel, Steve. "Guard Members Leave for 9 Months in Bosnia," *Washington Post*, Thur, 3 Feb 2000, p. B1.

Von Hippel, Karin. *Democracy by Force: US Military Intervention in the Post-Cold War World*. New York: Cambridge University Press, 2000.

Winograd, Erin Q. "Army Likely to Alter War Reserves In European Theater," *Inside the Army,* 13 August 2001.

Wolfe, Frank. "Joint Task Force To Direct Pentagon's Cyber Defense," *Defense Daily* (26 January 1999), p. 1.

_____. "Optempo May Drive Navy To Seek More Ships," *Defense Daily* (16 June 1999), p. 5.

_____. "Zinni: Strategic Mobility CENTCOM's Greatest Need," *Defense Daily,* 2 March 2000, p. 3.

Wolfson, Adam. "How To Think About Humanitarian War," *Commentary* 110 (July-August 2000), pp. 44-48

Wood, David. "Need For MPs Spurs Debate," *Army Times,* 27 Mar 2000, p. 16.

Woolley, Peter J. "Geography Revisited: Expectations of US Military Intervention in the Post-Cold War Era," *Peacemaking, Peacekeeping and Coalition Warfare: The Future Role of the United Nations,* edited by Fariborz L. Mokhtari. Washington, DC: National Defense University, 1994.

Worley, D. Robert. *Challenges to Train, Organize, and Equip the Complete Combined Arms Team: The Joint Task Force.* IDA paper P-3431, September 1998.

Wynn, Donald T. "Managing the Logistics-Support Contract in the Balkans Theater," *Engineer,* 30 (July 2000), pp. 36-40.

Zachary, G. Pascal. "Market Forces Add Ammunition to Civil Wars," *Wall Street Journal,* 12 June 2000, pp. A21-22, DL London.

Index

The Author

Frank Schubert was born in Washington, DC, and is a graduate of Howard University (BA, 1965), the University of Wyoming (MA, 1970), and the University of Toledo (PhD, 1977). He is a Vietnam veteran and worked as a historian in the Department of Defense for the US Army Corps of Engineers (1977-1989), the US Army Center of Military History (1989-1993), and the Joint History Office of the Office of the Chairman of the Joint Chiefs of Staff (1993-2003). He was a Fulbright scholar at Babes Bolyai University in Cluj, Romania, during the academic year 2003-2004 and has lectured at universities and research centers in seven European countries. Most of his published work has been on North American frontier exploration, black soldiers in the US Army, and military construction. Official publications include *Building Air Bases in the Negev: the US Army Corps of Engineers in Israel, 1979-1982* (1992) and *Whirlwind War: the United States Army in Operations Desert Shield and Desert Storm,* (general editor with Theresa L. Kraus, 1996). His most recent book, *Hungarian Borderlands: from the Habsburg Empire to the Axis Alliance, the Warsaw Pact, and the European Union,* was published by Continuum (London) in the autumn of 2011. He and his wife Irene divide their time between homes in Fairfax County, Virginia, in Győr, Hungary, and on Eagle's Nest Lake, Minnesota.

www.ingramcontent.com/pod-product-compliance
Lightning Source LLC
Chambersburg PA
CBHW080404270326
41927CB00015B/3344